The leaders of this new movement are replacing traditional liberal beliefs about tolerance, free inquiry, and even racial harmony with ideas so toxic and unattractive that they eschew debate, moving straight to shaming, threats, and intimidation.

– Matt Taibbi, Rolling Stone

THE WOKE SUPREMACY
An Anti-Socialist Manifesto

PREFACE

Just over a hundred years ago, three things happened almost simultaneously that created the modern world as we know it. The first was World War I, which left the most advanced cultures in human history physically decimated and financially bankrupt. Due to these cultures' embrace of this foolish war and, subsequently, their inability to extricate themselves from it, they were left with a form of governance that was no longer seen as viable.

Just in time to fill this void, two new systems of governance burst onto the world stage. These two systems – Socialism and Modern Nationalism (or just "Nationalism" from here on out) – are diametrically opposed and mutually exclusive and, because they are, they have spent the past hundred years vying – and often warring – for acceptance around the globe.

With the defeat of the German Socialists in World War II and the later collapse of the Soviet Socialist empire, it was generally recognized that this battle had been won and that Socialism was, as Ronald Reagan said it should be, on the "ash heap of history." Famed political philosopher Francis Fukuyama called it "the end of history," in that man's long struggle to find the best possible system of governance had finally ended with the unparalleled peace, prosperity, good health, innovation, and promise of America's Nationalist system winning out over the horrors and failures of the socialist world.

Socialism is back, however, and it is once again at war against Nationalism in general and America in particular.

I am of the belief that this war is going to get bloodier. If there is one thing the world should have learned at the most horrific of costs, it is that there is no appeasing Socialism. Socialism doesn't stop its invasions, oppressions, cruelties, and atrocities until it is forced to. There is no compromising with socialists. There can be no deals made with socialists and, if and when a deal is cut, socialists never intend to keep their side of the bargain. There is no truth in the words the socialist speaks nor does a socialist aspire to any good intentions beyond the "perfect world" their invasions, oppressions, cruelties, and atrocities are meant to create.

What that perfect world would look like has differed in the minds of the various socialist rulers of the past hundred years like Lenin, Stalin, Mao, and Hitler (as well as lesser socialist figures like Castro, Maduro and Kim) and it differs again with the Democratic Socialists of today. But, in their quest to create the perfect world they envision, they hold nothing sacred and believe no action is beyond the pale. Thus it was and thus it always shall be.

While the socialist of today will point to the Nordic nations as examples of where Socialism has worked, the Nordic states are, in fact, in no way Socialist. As I will show later in this work, they are *Nationalist* countries whose culture and economic model actually puts them fairly far-right on America's political spectrum. The use of these States as examples (while ignoring Nazi Germany, Soviet Russia, and Socialist China) is part of a bait-and-switch confidence game: the Left promises Denmark in the year 2020 but actually intends to remake America in the image of Germany of the 1930s, Russia of the 1940s or China of the 1950s with only different "heroes" and "villains" this time.

When people say that history repeats itself, they don't mean that it produces an exact clone. Instead, they mean that there are enough similarities in behaviors and practices to recreate the same outcomes time and again. In reading the following I implore both sides – those who would join with the Socialists in their war against America and those who would fight for America against this latest Socialist effort – to look for the similarities between the historical examples and today. They are, in fact, chilling.

Finally, I have made it a point, in every possible instance, to illustrate my case with the best-known examples and the most iconic quotations from the most central of history's figures. I do so because I can. The truth is often so obvious that it is well-known to all but gets lost in the "cleverness" and academic mumbo-jumbo far too many people then mistake for smarts.

In fact, in the hope of making my case undeniable, I have written this almost in the form of a primer. My ultimate purpose in creating this work is to convince those who mindlessly support the Left to give thought to the things they already know, while at the same time steeling the people who oppose this latest Socialist effort for the fight. If we are to fight, it is essential that both sides know what it is they're fighting for, how dire is the situation and what is likely to befall humankind if somehow, this time, the Socialists were to win.

INTRODUCTION

The mistake most people make in trying to understand Socialism is to think of it as an ideology. It is not. It is an economic model and a governing system that has been employed by any number of different ideologies over the past hundred years. Socialism is about the structure of money and power; ideology is about how that money and power is used.

This misconception has permitted the Democratic Socialists to get away with calling themselves a "different kind" of Socialist when, in fact, while their ideology may be different, there is no difference whatsoever in the Socialist structure they embrace.

This confusion has also allowed the Democratic Socialists to avoid taking an honest look at the very real similarities their movement has with some of history's most atrocious regimes by pointing to differences in their ideology. At the same time, it has left their opponents arguing points about their ideology that simply do not apply to the Democratic Socialists.

The first part of this work deals only with the Socialist *system*. It in no way seeks to draw a comparison between the *ideologies* of Hitlerism, Leninism, Stalinism, Maoism or the "ism" of your favorite professor or candidate. The discussion about ideologies comes later.

In fact, for now, I will stipulate that the ideologies of Hitlerism and Democratic Socialism are polar opposites. I offer this concession not simply to remove the indefensible from the discussion but because, in some of the most essential ways, it's true. Democratic Socialism was conceived of – or at least sold as – the antidote to Nazism and other supremacist ideologies that have caused humanity so much pain.

1

Whereas Nazism was about hate, Democratic Socialists were going to be about love. Whereas the Nazis marched in lockstep, they would walk to the beat of their own drums. Whereas the Nazis were uniformed and regimented, they would let it all hang out and do their own thing. Most importantly, whereas the Nazis committed the most egregious acts of discrimination, the Democratic Socialists were not going to discriminate at all.

That the ideology of Democratic Socialism is the polar opposite of Nazism, however, should not be as reassuring as it sounds.

For one thing, as I will show, ideology tends to have very little influence over behavior once the Socialist system has been embraced. Every Socialist regime has had an ideology that was at least somewhat different from the others; and yet, in practice, all of them have exhibited far too many of the same ugly qualities.

Further, polar opposites tend to have more in common with one another than they do with things more toward the middle. The North and South poles are quite literally polar opposites and, because they are, they are more alike than they are different.

Finally, being the polar opposite of Hitler, the Democratic Socialist shares with him a sense of supremacism. After all, if Hitler was the *worst* person to have ever lived, then they must be the *best* people to have ever lived, a claim not much supported by the evidence, but which gives the Democratic Socialist, in his mind at least, the moral authority to commit some pretty dastardly acts in the name of "anti-Hitlerism."

These things, however, are not for now. For now, it is stipulated that the ideology of Democratic Socialism is everything they believe it to be – the very antithesis of Nazism and the most loving philosophy mankind has ever devised. It is the Socialist *system* that's in question in the pages below.

HITLER WAS A SOCIALIST

Let's start with a fact so obvious that many Democrats no longer even bother to try and deny it: Hitler was a Socialist.

It is, after all, an awfully hard thing to deny when the name of the party Hitler led was the National Socialist Workers' Party and the government he ran controlled – either outright through ownership, or de facto via laws and regulations – every essential aspect of the German economy and culture. The latter, in fact, is the very definition of Socialism.

Rather than attempt to deny the undeniable, those on today's Left tend to argue that Hitler was the wrong "kind" of Socialist. Hitler, they say, was a "National" Socialist – the emphasis being on his Nationalism – while today's Leftists are "Democratic" Socialists and therein, they insist, lies all the difference.

If only they could recreate Hitler's many Socialist welfare policies – his nutritional subsidies, his environmental programs, his anti-poverty crusades and so on – but this time without his Nationalist fervor, they argue, the Socialist system will finally work and the utopia it has promised since Karl Marx first described his "workers' paradise" will finally and forevermore reign.

It is very much the same argument Bernie Sanders made about another Socialist regime during the 2020 Democratic Party Presidential debates when he repeatedly called for the recreation of Fidel Castro's literacy programs, only this time without all of that murder and oppression that that *third* "different kind" of Socialism brought.

The problem is that, while there are vast *ideological* differences between National Socialism and Democratic Socialism, there is simply no *systemic* difference between the two. The modifiers the Left uses to try and obscure this fact do not in any way alter the system they both equally embrace.

The word "Democratic" refers not to a social order or an economic model but only to the means by which various individuals intend to first come to power. Once empowered, the Socialist system of governance – outright control of all "essential" industries and de facto control over all of the others – remains the same. In fact, Hitler might well have called himself the "father of Democratic Socialism" since he, too, first brought his Socialist government to power through the democratic process.

At the same time, the fact that Hitler was a member of the *National* Socialist party no more proves him to have been a Nationalist than the fact that LeBron James plays basketball in the *National* Basketball Association proves him to be one.

James plays basketball not in a local or regional league – he's too good a basketball player to perform on such a limited stage – and so he plays basketball in a *national* basketball association. Hitler was a socialist not in a local or regional socialist party – he was too good a socialist for such a limited arena – and so he headed up the *National* Socialist party.

Hitler's movement wasn't the Nationalist-Socialist party; it was the National *Socialist* party, no more proving it to have been a nationalist movement than is the Democratic

National Committee, the National Academy of Motion Picture Arts and Sciences or the National Sewing Club for that matter.

SOCIALISTS ARE GLOBALIST

Hitler wanted to rule the world. People who seek one-world governance are called "Globalists." What they plan to do with the world can differ – and can differ greatly – depending on their ideology, but the desire for one-world governance, in any of its forms, is called "Globalism."

The people who defended their borders from Hitler were acting as "Nationalists." What these people intended to do with their nations varied – and varied greatly – depending on their ideology, but those who seek to preserve a world with fixed borders and local sovereignties are called "Nationalists."

That Hitler wasn't a nationalist should be obvious to even the most casual observer of history. In fact, one of the very first things Hitler did upon coming to power was to *destroy* the symbols of German Nationalism and replace them with the Swastika and other symbols of his greater ambitions.

Further, under Hitler's rule, it wasn't being a German that made one supreme – the souls of millions of German Jews and others attest to that. Nor did *not* being German prevent one from being considered a good Nazi.

When being a German offers no particular protections and not being a German comes with no disqualifying costs, it's hard to argue that Hitler was a German Nationalist. And, of course, he wasn't. He was a Globalist Socialist who, at least in these two basic and essential ways, was no different from Alexandria Ocasio-Cortez or your favorite barista at Starbucks today.

Not all Globalists are Socialists, but all Socialists are Globalists. In fact, Globalism is one of the defining traits of Socialism and is codified in the Socialists' founding document. This is why Marx made his ultimate call-to-action for the workers not just of Russia but of the entire world to "unite" in what he intended to be a global revolution.

While this "taking over the world" stuff might sound like the dreams of only madmen, sociopaths and megalomaniacs, and not at all what today's Socialists in America would want to do, it is, in fact, the endgame of every Socialist whether he screeches it with vicious vitriol like Hitler, delivers it in market-tested soundbites like Elizabeth Warren, or sets it to a happy tune like John Lennon.

In his song "Imagine", Lennon offers the three requisites for paradise common to every Socialist movement: that there be no personal possessions, no countries, and no religions.

The elimination of the individual's right to the fruits of their own labor is, in fact, the very centerpiece of the Socialists' cultural and economic model. The eradication of international boundaries is, of course, the essence of Globalism, while a bitter antipathy towards religion has been, and remains, a hallmark of the Socialists' efforts in every one of its ideological incarnations up to and including the Democratic Socialists of today.

According to the Socialist, these are the three basic requirements for the perfect society. Just what that perfect society would look like and what kind of people would populate it differs depending on ideology, but every socialist from Marx to Hitler to Lennon and those who sing his song today promised to create the perfect world of their imagination once these three preconditions had been met.

The problem is that the three requirements for the perfect world they each imagine are also the three requisites for the hellish world the Socialist system has never yet failed to bring in reality.

This is because, without possessions, the individual does not have the resources to stand up to a tyrannical government. Without nations, there are no other governments strong enough to challenge the Globalist rulers' every mandate while, without religion, there is no higher moral authority to countermand the rulers' every dictate, no matter how egregious and immoral those dictates might be.

How the Socialist intends to use this power differs – and can differ greatly – depending on the socialist's ideology but, to this point at least, there still remains no difference whatsoever between the system embraced by today's Democratic Socialists and the system employed by those who committed the greatest atrocities the world has ever known.

SOCIALISM'S ATROCITIES

Putting aside for the moment whether any one-world, godless society where food and clothing, houses and cars, iPhones and laptops, parts for machinery and the power to run them and all other essential means of production, distribution and storage is controlled by the government is even viable (spoiler alert: it's not), there remains the sticky business of how to first bring such a world about.

The reason Lennon's three-minute ditty remains so attractive to so many good people is that, because it is only a three-minute ditty, Lennon chose not to provide the specifics as to how he intended to bring his vision of heaven to earth. As always, the devil is in the details.

But, while we don't yet know *how* the Democratic Socialists intend to rid the world of its literally billions of people who believe in the right to the fruits of their own labor, the protections afforded them by national sovereignties and the moral codes that various religions bring, what we *do* know is that, in order to create the paradise they imagine, the Democratic Socialists will have to find *some* way to eliminate them. Put simply, in order for all the people to, as the song goes, "live as one," all of the *Others* need to in some way be dealt with.

SOCIALISM'S TECHNOLOGY

While the exact methods the Democratic Socialists intend to employ are not much discussed either in song, stump speech, or college lecture (such things are typically not much discussed until after the revolution has been won anyway) what we do know is how those who embraced the Socialist system have sought to accomplish it in the past.

The Russian Socialists chose gulags and work camps, permanent confinement to mental institutions, and exile to frozen tundra. The German Socialists opted for the more efficient and effective gas chambers and ovens, while the Chinese Socialists, seeking to save on infrastructure and material costs, went with mass starvation and other low-tech means.

While these kinds of atrocities are typically blamed on the *ideologies* of these various Socialist entities – giving comfort to some that "this time," with today's Socialists embracing a different ideology, things will somehow be different – the fact is that gulags, death camps, and killing fields are not ideologically-driven. Who is *sent* to them is.

Gulags, killing fields, and death camps aren't ends; they are the means to an end. And, as hard as it may be to believe, they are, in their essence, the same end Gal Gadot and all of those other lovely folks from TV and movies sang about: the creation of the perfect world of their imaginations.

Hitler didn't imagine a world of gas chambers and ovens; he imagined a world *after* the gas chambers and ovens had accomplished their purpose. Stalin didn't imagine a world of permanent exile and imprisonment; he imagined a "workers' paradise" once the Others had been effectively silenced. Mao didn't imagine a world with hundreds of millions of dead bodies littering the land; he imagined the perfect world that would come once the killing fields had done their job. If Stalin could have just blinked his eyes, if Mao could have just waved a wand, or if Hitler could have just snapped his fingers and accomplished the same ends, surely, they would have.

While today's socialists still can't just blink their eyes, wave a wand or snap their fingers, what they can do – and what they, in fact, do – is just flip a switch or write a couple of lines of code and thereby accomplish the same ends their Socialist predecessors sought to accomplish: the silencing of all the Others.

There's no doubt that the *means* the earlier Socialists used were infinitely more ghastly, but their purpose was one and the same. The gulags, killing fields, and gas chambers were simply the more technologically primitive tools of what today we call a "Cancel Culture."

11

This, in fact, is exactly what George Orwell was warning about in his book, *1984*. The genius of Orwell isn't found in his understanding of Socialism's inherent traits of authoritarianism and totalitarianism – these things were well known and well understood by everyone right from the start. In fact, Marx even wrote them into the very theory of the perfect Socialist society. The founder of the system embraced by Lenin, Stalin, Mao, and Hitler – and which the Left wishes to bring to America today – knew that, before the utopian world of the Socialists' imagination could even be tested, there would first need to be a vicious "Dictatorship of the Proletariat" to take care of the dirty work of cancelling all of the Others.

Just who those Others have been over the years has changed with each new ideology (and is different yet again today), but even in theory, Marx understood what had to be done before the utopia Socialism promises in one or another guise can first even then be put to the test.

Orwell's genius is found, instead, in his prescience in foreseeing how technology would become the new gulags and gas chambers; a less bloody but far faster, cheaper and more effective way for the next generation of Socialists to silence and disempower all Others in order to create whatever version of the perfect world was next time imagined.

Orwell wasn't warning about totalitarianism and authoritarianism in general, or even the specific ideologies of Leninism, Stalinism, Maoism, or Hitlerism – all of which occurred during his lifetime and offered him ample opportunity to tell their distressingly similar tales. Orwell was warning about the *system* of Socialism, no matter what ideology next came along to embrace it.

12

WHAT IS NATIONALISM

Nationalism is the only real-world alternative to Globalism. As such, it is the only real-world bulwark against the crimes and atrocities that the Socialist system requires and – no matter the many and varied ideologies that have embraced it – it has never yet once failed to bring.

This doesn't mean that Nationalism is not without its flaws or that as a system it can't be hijacked by a bad ideology. What it means is only that, over the past hundred years, in both theory and practice, Nationalism has proved itself to be the only thing that stands between freedom and the horrors of the Socialist economy, the globalist structure and the authoritarian and totalitarian practices required to bring those things about and then maintain them.

Those who attempt to denigrate Nationalism knowing that its failure is their success, typically do so by using an antiquated definition. When they attack Nationalism, they're referring to a time over a hundred years ago – before America arrived on the world stage – when monarchs and tsars and others of that ilk were seen as anointed by God. The loyalty of the people, then, was not to country and their fellow countrymen as it is today, but to the crown or another of the anointed.

In fact, when Democratic Socialists attack Nationalism employing this ancient definition, they are actually weakening their own case. In reality, the system they're attacking is far closer to the Socialism they're selling than it is to what Nationalism means today.

The Nationalist of old and the Socialist of today both embrace a system in which a venerated government owns everything within its realm. This is why the brilliant Thomas Sowell titled one of his most essential works describing the ideology of today's Left, *The Vision of the Anointed.*

What the Nationalist believes is that the world, with its eight billion people, seventy-two hundred languages, forty-two hundred religions and an incalculable number of further complicating factors such as varying climates, soils, topographies, natural resources and more, is simply too complex for the sort of top-down, one-size-fits-all governance that Globalism demands and for which Socialism provides the money and power.

The Nationalist believes that the best – the most effective, efficient, progressing, progressive, moral, and just – way of organizing the planet is through Nation/States where local leaders, with firsthand knowledge of local realities, create policy in the best interests of the local citizens they might then well run into on the streets.

Far from seeking the elimination of personal property, countries and religions, under the Nationalist system the people of each country are free to choose their own forms of governance, embrace the religions of their convictions and to pursue happiness as they define it, as they see fit and as their efforts will allow.

The fact that over the years, wrongs have been committed by Nationalists is not the lesson that should be taken from its history. To judge one idea by its imperfect real-world past while disregarding another's blood-soaked history in favor of a two-hundred-year-old theory and yet another imaginary ending is to disregard reality entirely and to court yet another nightmarish chapter in human history.

That such things as Colonialism, for example, can be ascribed to some who have embraced the Nationalist system is far less important to a mature understanding of history and as a lesson in how best to move humanity forward than the fact that such practices were long ago ended. Even more important is just how and why their ends came to be.

Since 1776 and the American Revolution, perhaps the most important of all Western colonies was India. With its abundance of teas and spices, silks and other cloths, as well as both overland and ocean trading routes convenient to the motherland in Great Britain, India was easily and by far the most valuable of all of the Western colonies.

Yet, not only did the British grant India its independence, it did so in response to one of only two great and successful *non-violent* movements of an otherwise very violent Twentieth Century. Mahatma Gandhi's campaign for India's independence succeeded – and could only have succeeded – because the appeal was made to Nationalists. This is because, while the only way to end the evils of the Globalist is to end Globalism, the best way to end the wrongs of the Nationalist is through a call to more and better practiced Nationalism.

Gandhi understood that Nationalism and Colonialism are diametrically opposed and mutually exclusive. He knew that one cannot at once embrace the tenets of national sovereignty while denying that right to others. He understood that, in order for there to be less of the evils of Colonialism, there had to be more of the good that is Nationalism. Gandhi knew that peaceful persuasion could work because, unlike Socialism, Nationalism doesn't require force to get others to do what they don't believe. He understood that all he had to do was convince the Nationalists to better practice the Nationalism they already embraced.

No similar call has ever or could ever work for those oppressed by Socialists because Globalism requires not just limited colonization but eventually the colonization of the entire world under a single government. That's the very definition of Globalism. Thus, while the "Western Colonialism" that today's Socialists use to attempt to discredit Nationalism was long ago and through peaceful means ended, Socialists continue to brutally colonize to this day.

THE WORLD AT WAR

With the defeat of Nazi Germany and the collapse of the Soviet Union, only two Socialist governments remain with sufficient manpower and resources to invade and oppress other peoples. One is Russia, which recently did what Socialists do and invaded and oppressed the sovereign peoples of Georgia and Ukraine. The other is China which, even as this is being written, is committing atrocities intended to deny freedom and sovereignty to the people of Hong Kong.

It is not a coincidence that those fighting for independence in Europe are allied with the Nationalist United States while those oppressing them are marching on the commands of a Socialist entity. Nor is it a coincidence that those fighting for their freedom in Asia are waving the American flag while those seeking to oppress them are marching under yet another Socialist banner.

Clearly the people of Hong Kong aren't waving America's flag because they're swearing their allegiance to the United States. They're waving America's Nationalist flag and singing America's Nationalist anthem because they understand that America's Nationalist symbols stand for the freedom, independence, and sovereignty they're fighting and dying so bravely to defend.

The Democratic Socialist understands what America's national symbols stand for as well, which is why, as freedom-lovers in Asia sing America's national anthem, the Democratic Socialist takes a knee in disrespect for it. It is why, as the people of Hong Kong wave America's national flag, the Democratic Socialists are burning it.

The battle there is the same battle here. It's the same battle that has been raging for the past one hundred years. It is a battle between the Socialist system of Lenin, Stalin, Mao, and Hitler and the Nationalist system that America first introduced to the rest of the world 100 years ago.

Until recently, what we've come to call the "Culture War" had remained relatively non-violent. For reasons explained forthwith and throughout, the hopes of its remaining so are dimming rapidly. Neither side makes any bones about its beliefs. One side shouts "make America great again" by rolling back Socialist advances that have destroyed the schools, hollowed out industry, and undermined freedoms, while the other argues that America is a "disease" and that only Socialism is the "cure."

Nor are the Socialists' anti-Nationalist ambitions hard to miss. For example, their flouting of immigration laws, hamstringing of those who would enforce those laws, and their efforts to first lure and then provide sanctuary to those who have broken those laws, may be a different *tactic* than using armies to invade Ukraine, but their goal – to eliminate an international border – is one and the same.

The Culture War is, in fact, a world war. Along with America, the battle to beat back Socialist oppression is taking place in Asia, much of Eastern Europe, and the whole of Western Europe where the people are trying to break free from the *supra*-national Socialist European Union. Where such battles for freedom against Socialist regimes aren't taking place – North Korea and Venezuela, for example – it is only because the governments there have so well succeeded in their relentless campaigns of oppression that opposition has been rendered futile.

From the Stars and Stripes being flown in Hong Kong, to the near mirror images of Brexit and the election of Donald Trump, as well as courageous (and thus vilified) leaders like Geert Wilders in the Netherlands and Marie Le Penn in France, Nationalism is at war once again with the same Socialist system it has been at war with since Socialism began its now century-old murderous run. Democratic Socialism is just the latest Socialist movement with One-World ambitions seeking to create the perfect society of their imagination through a Cancel Culture different this time only in its advanced technological sophistication.

SOCIALISTS CAN'T CO-EXIST

The fact that the Nationalist prefers a world with a multiplicity of countries, religions, and cultures puts the lie to two of the Democratic Socialists' greatest claims to moral supremacy. It is Nationalism, not Socialism, that seeks to live in peace and harmony with the other peoples and cultures of the world and, because it does, it is Nationalism, not Socialism, that promotes co-existence and diversity.

Globalism, by its definition, demands enforced homogeneity. One-size-fits-all policy requires all the people to either be of the same "size," oppressed into silence should they complain about "ill-fitting" policy, or cancelled entirely if they complain too loudly, too often, or too effectively.

Not long ago, the world had an unprecedented and near-perfect opportunity to test Nationalism and Socialism not in the classroom, a five-minute stump speech or a three-minute ditty, but alone and head-to-head on the world stage in real-time and with real-world consequences. The result determined the fate of hundreds of millions of human beings and still reverberates around the globe to this day.

At the end of World War II, with the German Socialists having finally been defeated in their quest to take over and homogenize the world, the nations of Europe were left devastated. Asia was in ashes, Africa remained a non-starter and the Muslim world was still primitive, violent, and self-destructive. Out of these ashes, the world was given the chance to start anew.

At that time, there were essentially only two systems contending for acceptance and only two nations with enough man-and-military power and resources to impose their will on others. One was Socialist Russia and the other was the Nationalist United States.

The Socialists wasted no time in doing what Socialists do: invading their neighbors, stifling dissent through oppression, atrocity and terror, and dictating universal policy for the entire Soviet bloc from their central location in Moscow. From there, the individualism, national sovereignty and religious choices of all the people were homogenized into a single Socialist entity they called the Union of Soviet Socialist Republics.

When, over the years, Nationalist independence movements arose in places like Hungary and Czechoslovakia, the Socialists were quick to put them down with even more brutal invasions, even stricter oppressions, still further atrocities, and even greater terrors.

Given that Globalists are, by definition, never content to simply rule a continent, the Soviet Socialists continued to attempt to spread their influence and ideology through invasion and atrocity, and via proxy throughout Europe, Asia, and beyond. These efforts didn't end until the moment of the Soviet Union's collapse in 1991 and even then, not without Russian tanks and gunners in the streets.

At this same time the United States, despite being in a far better position economically and militarily – and in sole possession of a weapon so powerful that the mere threat of its use would have seen other nations quickly capitulate – didn't seek to take over the world. In fact, the most powerful nation in the history of the world didn't even take over Canada or Mexico, despite both being right there on its border and both being ripe for the picking.

It is only due to America's embrace of Nationalism and the respect for other peoples and cultures Nationalism promises that – unlike Poland, Hungry, and the other nations of Eastern Europe and beyond – Canada and Mexico were, and continue to be free to choose their own unique forms of governance and embrace policies that may be, and often are, in opposition to the wishes of the United States.

While it is always fun – and often funny – to listen to the words of millionaire and billionaire proponents of Socialism who themselves then practice exactly the opposite of what they preach, it is far more enlightening to recall the *actions* of those who lived through these times and who actually had skin (quite literally) in the game.

In the seventy-five years since the defeat of the Germans, while millions of people have continued to flee every Socialist regime that has ever been, one can count on one hand the number of sane people who have fled America to make a new life for themselves in a Socialist land. Even those who make a grand show of promising to leave every time one or another election doesn't go their way never quite seem to make the move.

While to those who fled these Socialist lands, the "American Dream" would have been at that point mere rumor, when rumor turned to reality upon their arrival, they testified to America's greatness yet again by not returning to their homes or setting sail for another land. These tens of millions of people didn't just flee Socialist oppression; they embraced America's Nationalism and became Americans. In fact, once the truth was known, they then sent for their loved ones to join them.

These people weren't fools who were unaware of America's flaws; they were people who had experienced rather than just imagined Socialism and understood that in the real world, great doesn't mean perfect and flawed doesn't mean failed. And, they knew this not from some textbook, video game or TV show but from real life.

One of the great truisms of the past hundred years is that the only people who support Socialism are people who have never lived under it. Those who have endured its torments will risk everything to escape it and swear the oath, "Never Again."

SOCIALISTS ARE SUPREMACISTS

Given the Socialist system's unbroken history of economic failure and unparalleled human devastation, it may be hard to fathom why some would wish to try it again. Yet, clearly, they do. And the reason they do is simple: Socialists are Supremacists.

Every socialist has been convinced that the evils of his predecessors was due not to the system they employed but to the ideologies they embraced. Each then conjured a new, and in their minds, this time truly supreme ideology that, once fully implemented, would finally see the world "live as one."

Just who and what that "one" is has differed – and is different yet again with Democratic Socialism – but the universal embrace of the supremacists' perfect ideology is and has been from the start the final requisite for the various utopias every socialist in turn has promised.

Since this section deals only with the Socialist *system*, it is premature to discuss just who and what the "one" is according to those who have conjured this latest perfect ideology. For now, however, we can at least give them a name.

Whereas the Marxist Socialist believed the Supreme Trait – the characteristic that when shared by all the people would create the perfect world – was found in the "Worker" and the German Socialist believed it was found in the "Aryan," the Democratic Socialist is convinced that the Supreme Trait is found in those they call the "Woke."

SOCIALISTS ARE HATERS

Just as the Democratic Socialists have given themselves a name, they have also given a name to those who do not possess the Supreme Trait. This time the Supremacists have chosen to call the Others "Haters."

Hate, in fact, has nothing whatsoever to do with the system or ideology embraced by those who oppose the Woke Supremacy. It's just a word these newest supremacists have chosen to use to dehumanize and dismiss the Others in the same way the Woke's Democratic party forebearers in the South used the n-word to dehumanize and dismiss blacks and others use the word "kike" to dehumanize and dismiss Jews.

In fact, as one would expect of supremacists, it is the Woke who are driven by hate and it is hard to imagine anyone who has witnessed the attacks upon President Trump and his supporters who can conjure any word other than hate to describe it.

It is irrelevant to the discussion at this point whether one believes that those who disagree with the Woke deserve to be hated – every supremacist believes that the Others deserve to be hated. Besides, given the fact that everything from the Lincoln Memorial to tomb stones at veterans' cemeteries have come under assault in this latest wave of socialist violence, it is clear that Trump is not, in fact, the target of the new supremacists' enmity. America is.

Why the Woke so hate America is something we'll discuss in the section on ideologies below. What matters for now is that, along with sharing every aspect of Lenin, Stalin, Mao and Hitler's disastrous and murderous system, the Democratic Socialist shares with those who have committed the most ghastly crimes in human history a Supremacist ideology with a searing hatred for the Other.

In supremacist movements, hate is not just "a" force, it is *the* force – the atomic force – that keeps the movement together, gives it purpose, and provides its followers' lives with meaning. The supremacist has no greater calling, no higher standard and no closer relationship with anyone or anything than he does with his hate for those who do not share his Supreme Trait.

Orwell understood this, which is why the only humanity present in the daily lives of the English Socialists in the book *1984* is the "Two Minutes Hate", during which the otherwise lifeless let loose with a torrent of angst and vitriol for a mythical enemy the Powers-That-Be had conjured for just that purpose. In today's Socialist movement, it is hate for a fictionalized version of America created by the Socialist Powers-That-Be in the universities, media outlets and elsewhere, that gives the Democratic Socialist's life meaning and the Woke their only link to their fellow human beings.

Whereas Nationalism bonds people together by regional concerns, neighborly interests, and civic pride and duties, there is absolutely nothing that bonds a supremacist to his fellow supremacist except his supremacism.

The White Supremacist has nothing in common with another White Supremacist except the color of his skin. The proletariat has nothing in common with another member of the proletariat except that they're both proletariats. The Woke Supremacist has nothing in common with another Woke Supremacist except that they are both Woke Supremacists.

Democratic Socialists aren't bonded by common hobbies, enthusiasm over the same art or literature, camaraderie that comes from rooting for the same sports team, and certainly not by being fellow citizens of a city, state, or nation. A New Yorker who is Woke feels no closer to an Unwoke New Yorker than a Nazi from Berlin did to a Jewish Berliner or a White Supremacist from Alabama did towards a fellow Alabaman who was black.

Even the most powerful and essential of human bonds – those between family, friends, and neighbors – cannot withstand the atomic force of the Supremacist's hatred. The Woke Supremacist will stop talking to his parents, turn his neighbors in to the police, and literally "unfriend" his best friend if he discovers that any one of them fails to possess the Supreme Trait of wokeness.

Neither does the Supremacist have any professional goals or artistic ambitions beyond the spreading of his hate. Just as in *1984*, the *only* purpose of the Democratic Socialist's career and, in fact, his entire life, is the promotion of the Supremacy and its narratives.

Soon you will hear from the Woke's leading historians, academics, politicians, and journalists, all of whom acknowledge in their own words (and proudly) that the entire purpose of their life's work is to promote hatred for the Other and that they (proudly) have no personal or professional standard other than that which best promotes that hate. For now, simply consider the case of Nancy Spector, the curator of the once highly regarded Guggenheim museum in New York City.

Perhaps at some point in her life, Spector had a passion for great art. Seeking out, studying, procuring, and sharing the most beautiful of things was likely her professional, if not her life's, mission. Because it was, she could bond with other art lovers over their shared passion for the beautiful, and with her fellow New Yorkers over their common pride in living in a city where such beauty and sophistication were so readily at hand.

Yet, now in charge of that once fabulous museum with its glorious history and tradition – and armed with just about all of the money in the world thanks to the museum's many and wealthy patrons – rather than sponsor an exhibit of great artistic merit, Spector installed a toilet bowl made of gold in the museum's bathroom.

This "exhibit" is called "America" and what makes it "beautiful" to Spector clearly isn't its unique form and design, stunning contrasts in colors or any of the other considerations art lovers take into account when judging the great works. It's a working toilet bowl. What makes it "beautiful" to Spector is only the Woke Supremacist's singular and all-abiding hatred for those she considers to be the Other.

Today, Spector can no longer bond with her fellow art lovers; only with those who agree with her that hatred for America is "beautiful." She can no longer bond with her fellow New Yorkers; only with those who agree with her that hate for America is "sophisticated." Like all Supremacists, Spector's only civic, cultural and artistic bonds are all rooted in hate.

Spector's exhibit is reminiscent of a scene from the 1972 movie *Cabaret*. The film takes place just as the Nazis are on the cusp of coming to power. The cabaret singer is, just as I'm sure Spector is, as nice and charming as a person can be and just about the last person you'd think of when you think of a Nazi or a Nazi sympathizer.

The song he performs is a tender ballad about love, acceptance and tolerance and, as both comedic schtick and to make the point in the extreme, he's singing to someone dressed in a cheesy gorilla custom all dolled up and darling.

The song is called *If You Could See Her* and it really is quite loving, tender and moving until the entertainer sings the final line:

> *If you could see her through my eyes...she wouldn't look Jewish at all.*

There is, of course, nothing actually humorous about comparing a Jew to an animal, but the Germans in the audience all laugh and applaud. What makes it "funny" to them is the shared hatred the German Supremacists had for the Others of their time. Similarly, there is nothing beautiful about a toilet bowl; what makes it "beautiful" to Spector is the Woke Supremacists' hatred for the Others of theirs.

THE ONE-DROP RULE

In all Supremacist movements, loyalty must only, always and entirely be to the Supremacy. Thus, even the longest-serving, most-dutiful, most-beloved and most highly-respected Warrior for The Cause – whether that cause is Stalinism, Nazism or Woke Supremacism – is only one infraction away from being hated themselves.

Later you'll read the stories of Tammy Bruce, Bernard Goldberg and Lawrence Summers – a longtime leading feminist activist at the National Organization for Women, a twenty-nine-year veteran of *CBS News* and the president of Harvard University respectively – all of whom went, in an instant, from being amongst the most revered and respected heroes of those in the Woke movement to being cancelled by their best friends, longtime colleagues and fellow warriors. Their "crime" in every case was that they made the mistake of putting moral, journalistic or scientific standards ahead of the hate-filled narratives supremacies demand at all times.

For now, consider the case of *Tonight Show* host, Jimmy Fallon. Fallon, whose show was number one in the ratings at the time, did what late-night talk show hosts do in a normal society and booked one of the biggest names and most entertaining guests he could find. He then did what late-night talk show hosts do by being engaging, fun and funny. Fallon was warm and welcoming as he treated his guest in exactly the fashion he'd treated all of his other guests, and in the style that had made him number one in late-night in the first place.

The problem was that that guest was Donald Trump.

By the next morning, *Variety*, one of the two uber-powerful trade magazines for the entertainment industry, came out with a hit piece that set the tone and let all of Hollywood know what the Powers-That-Be in the Supremacy expected them to do.

Instantly, Fallon's fans, friends and colleagues turned on him. His ratings plummeted and his show quickly dropped to third, behind the two now more trustworthy voices of the Supremacy, Jimmy Kimmel and Stephen Colbert.

The same people who, just the day before, had begged to be on Fallon's show, blackballed and blacklisted him. Even today, almost half-a-decade later, Fallon remains unforgiven in Supremacist circles for the crime he'd committed against the Supremacy despite the numerous groveling mea culpas issued by the star.

The Supremacy didn't just chide Fallon; they did what they do to anyone and everyone who fails, even once, to be in the service of the Supremacy – they sought to destroy him. Here's Fallon, in his own words, responding to those who had been his friends and fellow warriors just the day before:

*I heard you. You made me feel bad. So now what?
Are you happy? I'm depressed. Do you want to push
me more? What do you want me to do? You want
me to kill myself?*

What Fallon had done that led him to believe those
closest to him might now want him to kill himself was a
late-night comedy show. What the Supremacy expected
him to do was their bidding. The word most often used
by his attackers for the "wrong" he had committed
was that, by treating Trump in the way the TV show host
treated any and all other people, Fallon had served to
"humanize" the Other.

Like the cabaret singer during the ascendency of the
Nazis, the late-night comedian must use his forum to
portray the Other as less than human. The Supremacy
demanded that Fallon treat Trump the way the
entertainer from a previous Socialist movement treated
the Jews. When he allowed it to be known that Trump
was, in fact, a human being, he faced the same kind of
wrath from the Supremacy that the cabaret singer would
have had he used his song to "humanize" the Jews.

SOCIALISTS ARE DEPLORABLE

Just as the Supremacy cannot allow for even one drop of
dissent from its followers, neither can it recognize even
one drop of decency in the Other. The Other cannot be
acknowledged to be a person of goodwill who just
happens to be wrong, or a decent person who is simply
misguided. He must be said to be, if not a subhuman
gorilla, then at the very least an utterly "deplorable"
human being (and "irredeemably" so, at that.)

In a Supremacy, the concerns of the Other must be said to
have no validity, and his motives no morality. At the same

time, he must be working as an agent for some massive conspiracy responsible for every ill the world has ever known and the cause of every one of the Supremacist's personal failures. In Germany it was the Jews who were the Others and therefore, at once, subhuman and in a global conspiracy; today it is the Unwoke.

Reasonable concerns about a crisis where hundreds of thousands of migrants are massing at the border – their health, history and intentions wholly unknown – must be declared by the supremacists to be "manufactured;" the Others' best efforts to mitigate the problem must be compared to "concentration camps," and its purpose must be said to be part of a global conspiracy of "White Supremacists" whose demise through any means necessary will end all of the world's problems and the supremacist's every personal woe.

Moral and practical qualms voiced by Others about even such extreme practices as "post-term" abortion – a euphemism for what is known in every other time and place as "murder" – must be dismissed as if wholly without basis, the Other said to be in a "war on women" and all of it part of a grand plot by an evil conspiracy of the all-powerful "Patriarchy," whose demise will end all of the world's sorrows.

Even undeniable scientific works from those only recently held in the highest esteem – including the very founders of a science the Supremacy has co-opted for itself, climatology – should it offer even one-drop of challenge to the orthodoxies of the Supremacists, finds the science dismissed out of hand, the scientist deemed the moral equivalent of a Holocaust-denier and the whole issue sold as the cunning work of a global conspiracy they call "Big Oil."

As supporters of the Supremacy, the Woke in political office no more feels a responsibility toward the Others in their jurisdiction than a government official in Nazi Germany, Maoist China or Stalinist Russia felt toward the Others of their times.

When the Speaker of the United States House of Representatives, Nancy Pelosi, says, "If there's some collateral damage to some who do not share our views then so be it," she is not just callously dismissing the destruction of the lives of former friends, neighbors and colleagues; she is casually dismissing the destruction of people she has sworn an oath to protect from the very kind of supremacy she has joined.

As globalists, Woke Supremacists don't see themselves as Americans; they see themselves as "Citizens of the World," and thus not bound by any nationalist document, law, oath or constitution. As Supremacists, their allegiance is only to those who possess the Supreme Trait, no matter in what country they may live; their enemies are anyone and everyone who does not possess this trait without regard to any other consideration save perhaps expediency.

Whether it's Pelosi putting policies that fund the invasion of America by illegal aliens ahead of the health, safety and well-being of the people of her district or Barack Obama weaponizing government agencies like the IRS and the FBI against fellow Americans who don't share his Supremacist views, the Woke in the field of governance have no higher calling, greater professional standard or other personal allegiance than the Woke Supremacist in any other field or endeavor.

In fairness, Pelosi did offer a slight caveat at the end of her declaration. She said that the destruction of the lives of innocent Americans who don't share the Woke Supremacists' views "...must not be our Original Purpose." And it's not. The cancelling of the Others is never the Supremacists' Original Purpose. It wasn't Lenin's Original Purpose; it wasn't Mao's Original Purpose and it wasn't Hitler's Original Purpose. The creation of the perfect world of their various imaginations has always been.

In fact, it is specifically because these crimes and cruelties *aren't* their Original Purpose that so many good people have done and continue to do so many bad things in every Socialist effort to date. Since their Original Purpose is the perfect world, they don't much consider the cruelties of their real-world actions. It's why Lennon left them out of his song.

WOKE UBER ALLES

As with those in all other Supremacist movements, the Woke Supremacist believes that all rights, opportunities and protections are to be afforded only to those who share the Supreme Trait. All Others are not only to be denied them but they can and must be harried, badgered, attacked and assaulted whenever and wherever they are found.

Powerful leaders in the Woke Supremacy like Obama and Maxine Waters, incite their fellow Supremacists to "get in their faces," and "let them know they're not welcome here." Others, like the Woke Supremacist governor of New York, Andrew Cuomo, eliminate the middleman and tell the Others straight out that "they have no place in the state of New York."

Like blacks in the Old South, the Other is denied service at coffee shops and restaurants, have their food spat on and even poisoned by Supremacist waiters while men, women and children are harangued, harassed and forced to flee for their lives if they sit down for a family dinner in a public restaurant.

As in all other Supremacist movements, any charge levelled against the Other – no matter how ludicrous the claim and no matter how cretinous the claimant – is immediately accepted as gospel by those in the Woke Supremacy.

Whether the accused is the President of the United States, a three-star General, a nominee to the Supreme Court or just a kid from Covington, Kentucky, and whether the accuser is a conman, a prostitute, a radical or a terrorist, the Supremacist convicts upon accusation and the Other can mount no effective defense.

Just as with blacks accused of a crime in the Old South, the accuser doesn't need to know where, when, who or how or have any corroborating evidence or witnesses in order to be 100 percent "believed" by their fellow Supremacists. Conversely, no charge against those with the Supreme Trait, no matter how egregious the crime, no matter how overwhelming the evidence and no matter how numerous and credible the witnesses, will ever see justice served.

THE MINISTRY OF TRUTH

While those who now control nearly all electronic interpersonal and political communications don't quite yet have the power to imprison those who speak against the Supremacy, they can and do "shadow ban" them and put them in *Facebook* jail.

This silencing of dissent effectively provides the new Supremacists with the same service that Stalin's gulags and Hitler's death camps provided, but in a faster, cheaper and more efficient way. The fact that it is less bloody is, of course, a plus, but the fact that it doesn't require train tracks, guard towers and gas chambers also allows it to be more stealthily conducted, more easily denied and more affordable to the Supremacists long before the revolution puts the money and power of government fully in their hands.

Whether or not this electronic ghettoizing of the Other as the Woke continue to promote their dehumanization is just a waystation on the path to a more final solution is a question that should not be dismissed. It's happened with Socialists before and more and more "highly respected," tenured and peer reviewed Woke Supremacists are publicly calling for just this and, even more chillingly, doing so without the slightest rebuke from their own.

The decision as to who and what is to be cancelled is said to be based on "community standards" but, as we have seen, Supremacists have no community except other members of the Supremacy, and they have no standards except those things that are best for The Cause at any given moment. Should a beloved member of the "community" at some point commit the crime of doing their job according to the standards as written for show, this friend and colleague immediately joins the ranks of the "Haters" and is cancelled forthwith and without defense.

All of this is more than just reminiscent of Orwell's *1984*, the apparatchik of the Supremacy at places like Facebook, Google and Twitter have exactly the same job that Winston had in the Ministry of Truth: combing through communications and shoving down the "Memory Hole" anything and everything that doesn't comport with the narratives and orthodoxies of the latest Socialist Supremacy.

THE MINISTRY OF INDOCTRINATION

The methods of silencing dissent are only slightly different on the Leftist-run college campuses where the Woke Supremacists forcibly shut down every idea that even hints at a challenge to the orthodoxies of the Woke.

One way they accomplish this is through a scheme the Supremacists have given the Orwellian name "Free Speech Zones." These are miniscule slivers of turf, often only about a yard wide, on the furthest reaches of the campus, where there is no one to speak and no one to be spoken to.

These are the *only* places on the campuses the Democratic Socialists run where those who do not walk in utter lockstep with the Supremacists may speak their minds without being officially branded "Haters" and, in turn, cancelled through intimidation, violence or decree.

Even then, these universities often require "pre-registration" for the opportunity to use these "zones," not because they are so highly in demand, but so that the Others know that the Powers-That-Be have their names on file and to put the "Hater" on notice that, from then on, he'll be being watched.

On the remaining 99.9 percent of the campus, the Supremacists deny the Other the opportunity to be heard by employing yet another twisted conceit. In a slogan that could be straight out of Orwell's Socialist dystopia, the Woke Supremacists have decreed that "Hate Speech Isn't Free Speech."

Since, in the binary world of the Supremacy, anything that isn't "woke" is "hate," there is literally nothing allowed to be said that offers even one drop of counterpoint to the unrelenting propaganda of the Supremacist administrators, professors, teaching assistants, students and any and every other voice given sanction to be heard.

In fairness, given their youth and the fact that the university is acting in *loco parentis*, the Powers-That-Be may give the young Other one last chance to swear allegiance to The Cause before his cancelling through expulsion. Before the final execution of the orders, the young Other may be offered a deal. If he'll agree to walk quietly into what other Supremacist movements have more forthrightly called "reeducation camps" but which today's more clever Supremacists have given the oxymoronic name "Tolerance Training," he may be allowed to continue on in his schooling – or, more accurately, his being schooled – so long as he issues a Soviet-style public apology and swears an oath to never again voice even one drop of doubt about the Supremacy, their words, their policies or their deeds.

BROWN SHIRTS AND LOAFERS

Wherever you find Supremacist movements you'll find the quasi-independent military wing charged with doing the dirty work that would be unseemly for the Powers-That-Be to be caught doing themselves. The Socialists of Nazi Germany called them "Brown Shirts;" the Democrats of the Old South called them the "Ku Klux Klan," and the Democratic Socialists call them "Antifa" and "BLM" today.

While the politicians, academics, media and the other Powers-That-Be in the Supremacy maintain a degree of plausible deniability by keeping their public efforts limited to incitement, the thugs are confident in their orders and the tacit understanding that they won't be stopped beforehand nor punished afterward.

It was exactly this deal that was struck between the thugs of Antifa and the Woke Supremacist mayor of Portland, Oregon, Ted Wheeler, that resulted in the near-death and permanent brain damage of journalist Andy Ngo. Technically, Wheeler didn't *order* the smashing in of Ngo's skull; he just let it be known in advance that *if* Antifa *were* to smash in his or anyone else's skull, he would order – and he did order – the police to stand down.

This is the same deal that the Woke Supremacy's leaders across America have made with the quasi-independent groups wreaking havoc today as the Powers-That-Be order the police to stand by and watch as the terrorists destroy the symbols of America's Nationalism and replace them with the symbols of the Supremacy's greater ambitions. It is the same deal Democratic party mayors are making in city after city where their efforts to defund the police ensure their thugs can't be arrested and their setting bail at zero guarantees they'll be back in the fight quickly if somehow one of them is. Meanwhile, in the absence of police protection, the "community" will do the policing but, of course, the only community Supremacists have is with their fellow Supremacists, and the only standards they'll apply is whatever is best for the further rise of the Supremacy.

SUPREMACISTS HATE AMERICA

There have been any number of Supremacist movements over the years, all of which have had one more thing in common. While they all had different traits they believed made them supreme, they all knew that America was their enemy.

The White Supremacists of the secessionist south, the Japanese and German Supremacists in World War II, and more recently, the Islamicist Supremacists like Iran, ISIS and al-Qaeda all join with the Woke in their recognition that America is the single greatest impediment to their various supreme ambitions.

Just as the people of Hong Kong recognize that it is America's Nationalism that is the opposite of Socialist Supremacism, every Supremacist understands that Nationalism and Supremacism are diametrically opposed and mutually exclusive.

Whereas the Supremacists' ideal is for all rights and protections to be afforded only to those with the Supreme Trait – whatever that Supreme Trait is according to that particular ideology – the Nationalist's ideal is to afford all rights and protections to every citizen equally and without regard to any other trait or traits.

This doesn't mean that America's Nationalists have always perfectly lived up to their ideals and the fact that such things as Jim Crow and segregation were tolerated for as long as they were makes this abundantly clear. Far more important to a mature understanding of history and as a lesson in how best to move humanity forward than the fact that these abhorrent practices once existed, however, is that they were long ago ended. Even more important is to understand just how and why their ends came to be.

Along with Gandhi's campaign for independence in India, the only other great and successful non-violent movement of the 20th century was that of the Reverend

Dr. Martin Luther King, Jr. Like Gandhi's, King's efforts could only have succeeded because he made his case to a Nationalist people.

Just as Gandhi understood that Nationalism is antithetical to Colonialism, King understood that Nationalism is antithetical to racism. He understood that, unlike the Woke Supremacists, he didn't have to use violence and intimidation to force people to accept things they didn't believe; he only had to convince them to better practice what they, as Nationalists, already embraced.

Individual acts of racism most surely do still exist in a Nationalist system – people can be such jerks; but because rights in a Nationalist system are based on citizenship, appeals like King's can be won and won peacefully. Any similar effort in a Supremacist society like that of the Socialist, would have no more succeeded than if Jews had peacefully protested for equal rights as German citizens, if a member of the bourgeoisie led a march for parity based on his Russian nationality in Russia, or if those who do not possess the Supreme Trait sought equal treatment in San Francisco, Portland or on any college campus in America based on the Constitution. Racism in America is episodic and anecdotal; the remedy to racism is institutionalized and systemic.

SOCIALISTS DON'T PEACEABLY ASSEMBLE

Perhaps nowhere are the equal rights afforded by the Nationalist and the total rights demanded by the Woke Supremacist so clearly on display as they are in how the two sides protest what they equally believe to be their rightful and righteous grievances.

Nationalist gatherings are peaceful and peaceable – even joyous. Riots are unheard of, and looting is not even a thought. (In fact, the Nationalists don't even litter, typically leaving streets cleaner than they were when they got there.) America's Nationalists file the proper paperwork, stay in their assigned areas and do not seek to block the right-of-way of others, either on the sidewalks or in the streets.

At Nationalist rallies, counter-protesters enjoy every right, privilege, freedom and protection afforded to every other citizen, and there are no crimes committed against others or their property at even the most well-attended (and well-armed) Nationalist gatherings.

The "protests" of the Woke Supremacists, on the other hand, are nothing less than scripted to be violent – and the more violent, the better. Riots and looting are pretty much a given, with the Powers-That-Be keeping their hands clean by limiting their overt involvement to inciting rhetoric, but quietly paying the bail of the Supremacists so the rioters can quickly return to the battle and supplying pallets of bricks so they'll be well-armed upon their return.

All Supremacists target first and foremost the most cherished icons of the Other. Thus, in the latest round of Supremacist violence, it was the Lincoln Monument and the Vietnam War Memorial that were viciously vandalized within the first days. Those who couldn't make it to Washington had to satisfy themselves with destroying more local shrines to America's veterans and other American heroes, with not even those in cemeteries allowed to rest in peace. Not surprisingly, then, these most recent Supremacist riots are more reminiscent of the Nazi's Kristallnacht than an actual "protest."

For reasons discussed toward the end of this work, Jew-hatred is central to all Supremacist movements and to

Socialist Supremacists in particular; and so, it is unsurprising that a favorite target of the Woke Supremacists are synagogues and Jewish shrines. Nazi-inspired propaganda promoting the same blood libels as their Socialist predecessors pop up at Woke Supremacist rallies, no matter the supposed issue behind the "protest" du jour. BDS – a movement created to finish Hitler's work by strangling half of the world's remaining Jews to death economically through boycotts, divestment and sanctions – is always prominently featured, no matter the supposed grievance being used to give the Supremacy cover on that day.

Even the lesser "protests" by the Woke Supremacists are intended not to rally the faithful through affirmation of their policy or persuade others to join them through reason and example but rather to use harassment, violence and intimidation to deny Constitutional rights to Americans who don't support the Supremacy.

The organizers of these assaults make no effort to disguise their purpose as they shut down those who, like Ben Shapiro, Charlie Kirk or Candace Owens, wish only to exercise their freedom of speech and physically attack those who wish only to assemble peaceably to hear them. Like the Nazis, the Soviets and Ku Klux Klan before them, Woke Supremacist "protests" are meant to frighten, intimidate, coerce, harass, badger, bully and beat into submission those who, through nothing more than their willingness to listen to another point-of-view, have failed the "one drop" test.

The Nationalist no more likes the Woke Supremacist than the Woke Supremacist likes the Nationalist. The difference is that, because the Nationalist is a Nationalist, he extends all the rights of a citizen to every citizen, even to those he most deeply disdains. Because the Woke Supremacist is a Supremacist, no allegiance, no oath and no standards apply, no laws are applicable to him, nothing is deemed sacred and even less is beyond the pale. In a Supremacy – any Supremacy – all efforts are meant only to deny the Others any rights, any comforts and any voice on their way to creating the perfect world the Supremacist this time imagines.

SOCIALISTS CANNOT LIVE IN PEACE

The same belief that sees Supremacists deny their fellow citizens equal rights at home is what leads Socialist governments to invade, oppress and commit atrocities against those in other lands. Nationalists don't invade their neighbors, either at home or abroad, and expect not to be invaded themselves. That's what Nationalism is. The Socialist, on the other hand, is mandated by his globalist beliefs to invade and compelled by his Supremacist convictions to oppress those who do not share the Supreme trait throughout his domain. Since the Socialist is a Citizen of the World, he believes the entire world is his domain.

This is why, in the strikingly short history of the Socialist system, invasion by one or another Socialist entity has been a constant. In just the one hundred years since Marx's theory was first put into practice there have been three Socialist governments with the manpower and the resources to invade other lands. Two – Germany and Russia – tried to take over the world, committed the cruelest of oppressions, and murdered more human beings than any other peoples in history.

The third, China, has been only somewhat less adventurous overseas, but this is mostly because, with a population of 1.4 billion people and provinces so different from one another they are akin to their own countries, the Chinese are typically still too distracted trying to homogenize their own people into one to venture too far outside their own already massive borders. Still, their body count is staggering – between 40 and 80 *million* people under Socialist favorite Mao Tse-Tung alone.

The history of the United States during this same period has been exactly the opposite. Not once in the past hundred years has America invaded another country for the purpose of conquest, treasure or glory. This is because, as Nationalists, Americans respect the borders of other nations and expect their borders to be respected in return. That's the very definition of the Nationalism they embrace.

While the history of the world prior to the modern era is not the purview of this work and thus will be left to others, it should be noted that whatever wrongs one ascribes to America prior to the Modern era were not the result of the Nationalist system but the failure of those who committed those wrongs to live up to the Nationalist creed. Each of these wrongs, were and could only have been remedied by the more and better practice of Nationalism and, unsurprisingly, then, were the acts – and, in fact, the official policy – of the same Democratic party that opposes the embrace of Nationalism today.

From the dawn of time until America's rise to power, invasion for treasure, glory and empire was simply the norm across the globe and across all cultures and civilizations. Yet, over the past hundred years, America, despite its unparalleled economic size and strength, has never once entered a war for any reason other than to stop the further spread of one or another globalist Supremacy and their atrocities.

Why it is that it is America who has had to step into the fray each time is very simple: because of the devastation wrought by those who had embraced the failed systems of Socialism and its predecessors and because of the success of America's Nationalist ways, only America has had the power to do so.

For the first seventy-five of the past hundred years, the Supremacists America has fought was one or another Socialist entity. World War II was fought to stop the further spread of Hitler's Socialist regime, while the Cold War was fought to prevent the further expansion of the Russian Socialist empire. The Korean war was fought to stop the proxies of the Chinese Socialists from overrunning their brethren to the south, while the Vietnam war was fought against the Soviet Socialists' proxies for the same reason.

Woke historians who, as we shall soon see, proudly admit that their job is no more to be actual tellers of truth than Spector's is to be a purveyor of beauty, use their profession to try and damage America's image by ascribing evil purposes to what were truly noble and heroic sacrifices. Every one of their claims is so easily debunked, however, that they know that their only hope of selling it is to make their lies big, to keep telling them and to make sure no other voice but theirs is ever allowed to be heard.

The Supremacy's propagandists don't so much *argue* their case as just throw out one or another buzzword – "imperialism," "racism," "greed" and the like. Those who have been long-steeped and wholly surrounded by the narratives and the orthodoxies of the Supremacy simply then take these charges as givens with no further questions asked. Simply to ask a question, they know, is enough to qualify one for the cancelling.

These buzzwords – much like the slogans Big Brother plastered everywhere throughout Oceania – instantly accomplish the Supremacists' goal of rendering the real and righteous concerns of those who supported the wars wholly without merit, those who chose to fight them deplorable, and those who ordered them leaders of one or another all-powerful and all-evil conspiracy.

What is most distressing about these false accusations is not that they're made by the Supremacy's Powers-That-Be – one expects those who are profiting the most from a movement to be the most corrupt and for the True Believers to be the most willing to lie on its behalf – but rather that such shallow and obvious lies, easily disproved with knowledge already in the possession of the people, are so readily and mindlessly embraced by the rank-and-file who enable and support the Supremacy.

It is this mindless acceptance of the narratives and orthodoxies of a Supremacy that most struck the famous political philosopher, Hannah Arendt, who, reporting on the trial of the very architect of the Holocaust, Adolf Eichmann, wrote that what was most terrifying was his "normalcy," and what was most chilling was "the banality of evil." The real threat in a Supremacy is not the ten percent or so who are the True Believers and the Profiteers, but the other ninety percent who mindlessly accept, repeat and act upon their narratives.

All one need know to wholly debunk the Woke Supremacists' narratives of "imperialism" and "greed," for example, is what transpired after the wars were either won or lost. Whenever and wherever the Socialists won – even if only temporarily – the result was the usual atrocities and brutal oppressions required by Socialist theory and employed by every Socialist regime. Conversely, whenever and wherever America was victorious, the result was a people soon free to decide their own forms of governance and to live by the culture, religions and practices of their choice.

45

When Hitler's Socialists invaded France, for example, the French were oppressed, brutalized and forced to follow Germany's every dictate. When France was liberated by American forces, they were then free to form their own government and embrace policy so often in opposition to that of the United States that one might think its purpose is little other than to be a thorn in America's side.

Similarly, when the Soviet Socialists controlled the nations of Eastern Europe, the people were brutalized, oppressed and forced to live by Russia's every command. When America won the Cold War and these nations were freed, every one of them became independent and sovereign states with their own forms of governance, unique policy, distinct cultures and various religious ways. In fact, as always, the only threat to their continued independence comes not from the United States or any of their Nationalist neighbors but only from the Socialists in Russia.

Charges leveled by the Supremacy that America's wars were fought because Americans are "racists" are even more easily debunked than the others. Consider the accusatory lyrics by Woke Supremacist favorite Bruce Springsteen, in his song about the Vietnam war, "Born in the USA":

> *Got in a little hometown jam/so they put a rifle in my hand/sent me off to a foreign land/to go and kill the Yellow man...*

According to Springsteen's tale, there were no legitimate reasons for fighting the war. The people who signed on to fight it, then, were racists and the government that ordered it had to have been part of an evil conspiracy seeking to spread the "White Supremacy" to Asia. In fact, those who side with such Supremacies often chant "One-two-three-four, we don't want your racist war."

The problem is that not only is Springsteen wrong, he is as wrong as wrong can be. His conclusion is as far from the truth as a toilet bowl is from beautiful and Jews being subhuman is from funny. More troubling than his being so wrong, however, is that Springsteen apparently didn't feel the need to give the matter even a moment's thought before leveling such a serious and damning charge against his onetime friends, neighbors, colleagues and country-men.

A moment's thought is *literally* all it would have taken. However ignorant of history Springsteen may or may not have been, he most certainly had to have known that, while it's true the people of North Vietnam the Americans were battling had "yellow" skin, so, too, did the people of *South* Vietnam for whom and with America was fighting.

And, no matter how dim-witted Springsteen may or may not be, surely, he then could have made the mental leap to the fact that, if both sides had "yellow" skin, then *obviously* the reason for the war couldn't have been the race of the peoples fighting it.

If Springsteen had bothered to give the subject even a moment's thought, in fact, he would have seen that America fought the Vietnam war to *protect* the "yellow" man (and the world) from the further spread of history's most murderous system, the same system that had only then recently brought the world Adolf Hitler and which the Democratic party he affiliates with seeks to bring to America today.

In fact, by taking the side of the North Vietnamese, the Woke Supremacists actually *caused* the deaths of millions of "yellow" men, women and children as, when their protests forced American troops to withdraw from the region, the Socialists of North Vietnam did what Socialists do and invaded, oppressed and committed the most

47

ghoulish of atrocities against the "yellow" people in the south.

While the willfully ignorant mindlessly repeat the narratives of the Supremacy (no matter the Supremacy), it is those who create these narratives who have the most blood on their hands. To those in the know, the deaths of and atrocities against millions of people with "yellow" skin in the South was not their Original Purpose; they were just seen by them as "collateral damage" in their war against America. "Yellow" lives didn't and don't matter to the Supremacists and the Powers-That-Be dismissed their deaths with the same imperious wave of the hand as Pelosi does to the innocent victims of the Socialist's war against America at home.

Meanwhile, when those who share Springsteen's ideology, political party and mindless acceptance of the Suprem-acy's narratives and orthodoxies met the men and women who had risked and sacrificed so much to protect the people of South Vietnam, they did what Socialists do and harangued, harassed and bullied them, calling them names, spitting in their food and faces and letting them know "they're not welcome here."

It is not surprising, then, that those American veterans who have suffered the most in the aftermath of a war are those who fought for freedom during the Woke Supremacist era. It is not surprising that the Democratic Socialists took the side of the invaders and oppressors in that war no matter how or how many "yellow" people died at the hands of the their fellow Socialist/Supremacists nor is it surprising that these same supremacists invade and oppress their fellow Americans at home. It's what social-ists – Supremacists all – do.

SUPREMACISTS UNITE!

With first the defeat of Hitler's Socialist regime and then the demise of the Soviet Socialists' brutal empire (and with numerous and free nation/states then filling the void) the world became more peaceful, prosperous and diverse than it had ever been – and not just by a little and not just in some places. The era of Socialist invasion, oppression and atrocity – the most murderous and horrific era in human history – had seemingly come to an end, and the world was enjoying the dividends that come from a world where nations respect each other's sovereignty and individuals are free to pursue their dreams as they see fit.

Today, with Nationalism having won out (at least for now), war – or even the threat of war – exists in only a handful of places. By no coincidence these are the places where the Nationalist system has not yet been embraced and where one or another Supremacist movement still holds sway.

Thus, in addition to the Socialist violence of the Woke Supremacy and the threat from Socialist regimes like those in Russia and China, about the only places where war remains a possibility is in Africa – where the system is "tribalism" and the Supreme Trait is "blood" – and the Middle East region, where the system is Islamicism and the Supreme Trait is extreme piety before Muhammad.

With Africa's geographic isolation and lack of oil or similar revenue sources seeing them still fighting with relatively primitive weaponry, Globalism is simply not a thought, much less a threat. While the family feuds on that continent can be brutal, the Supremacists in Africa do not and cannot seriously imperil the peace of the world and thus America, as Nationalists always reluctant to war, has had minimal involvement on that continent.

The story is very different in the Middle East region where the Islamicists are situated at the crossroads of three continents – Asia, Africa and Europe – sit on a staggering amount of oil wealth, which can and has been used both as a weapon and to purchase the most advanced weaponry, and where, because Islamicism is a globalist ideology, the threat to the peace of the world is very real and constant. It is for this reason, then, that the only wars America has been involved in since the demise of the Soviet Socialist Supremacy have been against one or another Islamic Supremacist movement or its rich and powerful enablers.

Not all Muslims are Islamicists – in fact, Muslims who fail the one drop test of that Supremacy are amongst the most oft and brutally targeted – but all Islamicists are Muslim. This, along with the fact that there's oil in the Middle East, has given the Woke Supremacist propagandists opportunities to throw out the usual buzzwords in their efforts to undermine America's reputation and prevent freedom's victory.

Woke Supremacists dismiss the legitimacy of the concerns of the Others as wholly without foundation by calling it a "phobia," and portraying the enemy as the "junior varsity," and thus not an actual threat. The people who support the actions are then deemed to be "racists" without a moment's thought for, with no legitimate reason to support the efforts, what other explanation could there be? As always, then, the whole thing is said to have been orchestrated by one or another all-powerful conspiracy of, take your pick, "Big Oil," "White Supremacy" or the "Patriarchy" (and its "toxic masculinity.")

These trite and hackneyed – rather banal – slanders are all just as easily debunked in these cases as they are when they're employed by the Woke's propagandists to disparage America's involvement in the wars to stop the supremacies of the 20th Century.

To dispatch with the charge of "racism" all one need know is that, while it's of course true that the Islamicists are Muslims, so too are the people America is fighting for and with to defeat them. Again, it is the Woke Supremacists in the know – people like Barack Obama – who wave their hands and say "so be it" as Muslims come under the brutal thumb of ISIS and the others. These Muslims, like the people of South Vietnam and the Unwoke in America, are just more "collateral damage" in the eyes of the new Supremacists.

"Imperialism" can just as easily be dismissed simply by knowing what transpired after the battles had been won or lost. As always, when the Supremacist movements like ISIS and Hamas won, the locals were horrifically oppressed, all forms of atrocities were visited upon them and all the people were forced to live as the "one" of that Supremacist ideology. Meanwhile, as always, where America won, the peoples were soon free to return to the practice of their religion and their ways of choice such as in Kuwait where the heredity-monarchy and Islamic (though not Islamicist) ways could not be more different than America's system and culture, but which were restored upon the victory of America and a coalition of Nationalist states.

The Woke Supremacists' charges of "greed" are even more easily debunked than the other two. All one need know to reject the Woke Supremacists' claims that these wars were fought to "steal their oil" is that Arab nations that have oil are staggeringly rich while Americans are still paying two, three and four dollars for a single gallon of gasoline at the pump.

The Woke Supremacist, of course, is just as well-aware of these obvious facts as Springsteen was that the South Vietnamese people had "yellow" skin; like their fellow supremacists, however, they simply do not give the narratives and orthodoxies in which they were steeped even a moment's thought.

If they did, it would be hard to imagine even a single one of them then mentally incapable of making the leap to the obvious: nations that have been plundered aren't rich and people who have plundered don't pay top-dollar for the things they've supposedly stolen. And, yet, every time, tens of thousands of the Woke Supremacists and their mindless enablers will show up at rallies, chant the most banal of slogans like "One-two-three-four, we don't want your racist war" and "No blood for oil!", promote the deaths of thousands of Muslims and the subjugation of thousands and thousands more and use America's "racism" as an excuse to promote even more Socialist violence.

THE SUPREMACISTS' ALLIES

The German Socialists allied with the Islamicists during World War II and the Soviet Socialists were the Islamicists' biggest financial, military and diplomatic benefactors throughout the Cold War. It should not be surprising, then, that the Democratic Socialists would side with the Islamic supremacists of today. Obama, for example, joined with the enemies of America by giving billions of dollars to the Ayatollahs and Mullahs in Iran, supporting the efforts of Hezbollah in Lebanon and ordering the military to "stand down" so the thugs of ISIS could do their work in Syria and beyond.

These alliances appear at first blush to be odd given that each of these Supremacist movements have a very different – in fact, typically diametrically opposed and mutually exclusive – Original Purpose. Hitler sought a world without Semites, yet Arabs are Semitic. Stalin sought a world without religion, yet the Islamicists are fanatically religious. The Democratic Socialists say they want a world without discrimination against women and gays, yet the Islamicists' subjugation of women and murder of gays is part of their Supreme Trait and is well-known to be by all.

The reason for these alliances, however, make perfect sense once one understands that, to a Supremacy nothing – nothing at all – matters except the Supremacy. The murdering of gays and the subjugation of women is not the Woke's Original Purpose. They too, however, are recognized by the Woke to be nothing other than just some more "collateral damage" in their war against America.

Each of these Supremacist movements knows that, before they can create the perfect world of their imagination, they must first destroy the world as it is. For this reason, just as no one in the service of the Woke will ever be brought to justice no matter how heinous their crime at home, no one will ever be opposed by the Woke Supremacist no matter how ghastly their atrocities or *who their targets* so long as it advances their agenda of destroying the world as it is.

Socialists – no matter the incarnation – and Islamicists are, in fact, very much alike. They are all globalist. They're all utopian. They all divide the world into only two kinds of people: those with the Supreme Trait and everyone else who they, in turn, despise with a seething passion.

They all embrace the belief that all rights and protections belong only to those who possess the Supreme Trait and they all subscribe to the one drop rule where the slightest impiety qualifies their best of friends, closest of colleagues and even parents, sons and daughters for the canceling. They all must use force to coerce, intimidate and terrify others into believing (or saying they believe) what they don't believe and, to all of them, nothing is held sacred and no target or tactic is beyond the pale in their march towards creating the perfect world of their various imaginations. This is why all of them have one more thing in common: they know that America is their enemy.

CONCLUSION

The newest Socialist is not an exact clone of all the others from the past. They never are. Yet, in every conceivable way, allowing for differences in technology, the new Socialist perfectly parallels the practices, purposes and even allies and enemies of those who embraced the system before him. To this point, it remains possible that, this time, the *ideology* of these latest Socialist/Globalist/Supremacists is truly the supreme ideology, and that their enemies, this time, truly are subhuman, evil and in a global conspiracy that is the cause of the world's every ill. In that claim, too, however, the Woke resemble every one of their predecessors.

WHAT IS WOKE

According to the Woke, the problem with all of those other Supremacist movements was that they each declared something – a person, a family, a race, a religion or a class, for example – to be better than everything else.

The Woke, then, are going to create the perfect world by going the other way. In order to create the perfect world of their imagination, the Woke have simply decreed that nothing is better than anything else. The Supreme Trait possessed by the Woke is total moral and intellectual indiscriminateness.

In the world of the Woke, all things – from behaviors to body-sizes, works of art and literature to systems of governance – are to simply be accepted as equally right, equally good, equally valid and equally true.

The Woke are convinced that, by eliminating discriminating thought, they will eliminate all of the evils of discriminatory practices. They believe that, by eliminating rational judgment, they'll eliminate all of the hurtfulness of judgmentalism and all of the harmfulness of prejudices. Their plan is to eliminate all of the wrongs of the world by eliminating the recognition of right and wrong itself.

Here's how Allan Bloom summed up Woke philosophy in his brilliant and essential book, *The Closing of the American Mind:*

> *All the world was mad in the past. Men always thought they were right and that led to wars, persecution, slavery, xenophobia, racism and*

56

chauvinism. The point [today] is not to correct the mistakes and actually be right, rather it is not to think that you are right at all.

If Bloom were writing today, he might have chosen a different word. What the Woke believe is that all of the people who ever lived were *asleep* – asleep and in some kind of fever dream that caused them to do all sorts of horrible things to one another for no good reason. Only *they* are awake – "woke" – and, because they are, they and only they in all of human history see the true road to paradise.

Since theirs is this time truly the perfect ideology, then of course it should be global in order to share the joys with all the world and to prevent the threat to their paradise that would come from any other ideology or system being allowed to remain. And, since theirs is truly the perfect ideology, of course all money and power should rest in their hands so that they can perfectly administer the perfect society and because, if it didn't, then those who are imperfect might have the resources to cause the same kinds of troubles that had plagued humanity until they came along.

The enemy of the Woke, then, isn't America alone – they simply recognize the same thing all other Supremacist movements have recognized: that destroying the Nationalist United States is the lynchpin to their further ambitions. Their true enemy is human civilization which, from its start, was filled with people who thought they were right and which, in turn, then led to everything that's wrong with the world from hurt feelings to holocausts.

Just as if the Nazis had won World War II or if the Islamicists had succeeded in creating their global caliphate, the Woke Supremacists seeks to eradicate from memory all things, good and bad, that existed before their rise. Anything and everything that mankind has created came from those who were "mad" or in some sort of fever dream and thus were less than fully human.

This is yet one more thing Orwell anticipated in the next Socialist society:

> *Every record has been destroyed or falsified, every book rewritten, every picture has been repainted, every statue and street building has been renamed, every date has been altered. And the process is continuing day by day and minute by minute. History has stopped. Nothing exists except an endless present in which the Party is always right.*

Orwell, of course, was *warning* about such a world; Lennon, on the other hand, was singing its praises. An "endless present" is *exactly* what Lennon promised the Woke paradise would be like when he asked everyone to "imagine all the people living for today."

AS WRONG AS WRONG CAN BE

There are, of course, a multitude of problems with an ideology where paradise requires no one to ever think they're right. One is that the Woke think they're right. Another is that the Woke are wrong.

But the Woke aren't just wrong; they are wrong about everything. All of the time. And to the Nth degree. This is neither because they're stupid (as in they lack either the knowledge or the mental capacity to arrival at the right and rightful conclusion) nor that they're evil. It is because the central tenet required to be Woke – the belief that nothing is better than anything else – is so fundamentally untrue that everything else that follows is not merely wrong but the very opposite of right.

In order to remain woke, one must undervalue the better; greatly undervalue the much better and undervalue most that which is the best of all. At the same time, they must overvalue the lesser, greatly overvalue the much lesser and most greatly overvalue that which is the least good, right, beautiful and true of all. In the end, such thinking might even someday see a people who put toilet bowls in their art museums and think of the greatest nation that ever was as a "toilet."

Most essentially to this work, the Woke are as wrong as wrong can be about the consequences of eliminating discriminating thought. By doing so, the Woke don't eliminate judgments; they simply turn *everything* into prejudice.

To conclude, for example, that America isn't exceptional is not have failed to make a judgement; it is to have judged America to not be exceptional. This conclusion, however, is pre-ordained and arrived at not through moral, scientific or experiential considerations but wholly devoid of them. Preordained conclusions arrived at without fact, reason or evidence is the very definition of prejudice.

Further, while others may have their prejudices, they may also sometimes be right. One can be both a "xenophobe" and correct in their belief that America is exceptional. The beliefs of the Woke, on the other hand, are not only all the product of their prejudgments but the Woke can never be right. This is because their purpose isn't to be right but to undermine the recognition of right and wrong by others.

In order to convince others to embrace their Supreme Trait (or at least to allow those who possess it to rule over them) they must make the case that the better isn't better and the lesser isn't lesser. This is their purpose so that all things appear to be equally right and equally true, the required belief to live as one of them.

Further still, while the prejudices of others can be remedied by the introduction of previously unknown facts, unexpected experiences or the presentation of a new and compelling line-of-reasoning, the Woke is immune to fact, reason and experience for these are the tools used only by those who intend to engage in discriminating thought. The Supreme Trait of Wokeness is the rejection of these things and thus, not only is everything they believe wrongful prejudices, but they are immovable. If the Woke were ever to be moved by these things, they would no longer be a member of the Woke.

Finally, it is this dedication to utter indiscriminateness that sees the Woke so convinced that everything from mathematics and grammar to the knife and fork are "racist." The argument the "best and the brightest" make about the fork, for example, is that, since there are other options – chopsticks or even fingers, for example – when someone chooses to use a fork, they have then made a discriminating judgment. Since the Woke must start and end their every belief convinced that nothing is better than anything else, then the only reason one would choose to use a fork is because they're bigoted. To the Woke, everything except indiscriminateness is "racist" because the opposite of indiscriminateness is discrimination.

THE ONE

Every society has its archetype; the iconic image of the kind of human being that that society needs and that every person should aspire to be. Some archetypes from recent American history include Rosie the Riveter, Norman Rockwell's depiction of the Boy Scout and Sloan Wilson and Nunnally Johnson's "man in the grey flannel suit."

Other societies have had their archetypes, too. The square-jawed and stoic, blonde-haired Aryan staring off into Germany's future; the lean and determined worker in the field from Leninist Russia; the humble, bearded and pious Islamicist and so on.

The Democratic Socialists have their archetype, as well. He is twenty-something, still sporting his baby-curls and without a wisp of facial hair that might hint at eventual maturity or, God forbid, masculinity. He appears to still be living in his parents' basement, clutching his only worldly possession – a cup of hot cocoa – so wholly without responsibility, desire or drive that he hasn't even bothered to change out of his night clothes. He's come to be known derisively as "Pajama Boy."

Pajama Boy wasn't the creation of the political far right meant to mock the moral and intellectual infantilism of today's indiscriminate Left. In fact, the model was chosen and costumed, the set was staged and lit, the nation's leading hair and make-up artists were called in and hundreds if not thousands of photos were shot before the Woke's top marketing gurus selected just the right image to connect with their core constituents in an effort to sell them on their flagship policy known as Obamacare.

What makes Pajama Boy the kind of person the Woke wishes to see everyone emulate is that, while chronologically he's a grown-up, in every other way he remains a child. To the Woke, the perfect adult – the Supremacy's version of the "worker," the Aryan or the pious Islamicist – is the permanent child in a grown-up body.

The hallmark of maturity is a growing desire, ability and responsibility to discriminate. Grown-ups must use their intellect and experience to seek out and procure the better things, for their ability to provide for themselves and their families and to contribute to the world depends on it.

To those who believe the perfect world is one without discriminating thought, infantilism is the ultimate attribute. For those who simply wish to foment revolution, the physically able but morally and mentally infantile is their perfect warrior: strong of body, easily controlled and, like everyone from Springsteen to Eichmann, wholly unquestioning. The Powers-That-Be in the Woke Supremacy know that, if this latest Socialist revolution is going to have its "useful idiots," how better to fill their ranks than by making the Supreme Trait idiocy itself?

This is yet one more thing Orwell anticipated, which is why, in order to convince the Socialists of Oceania not to question the narratives and orthodoxies of that Socialist government, he reminded them constantly that "Ignorance is Strength." To the Woke Supremacist, ignorance isn't only strength, it is the Supreme Trait.

Keep in mind that this ignorance isn't for lack of information – Springsteen knew that the South Vietnamese had yellow skin, while those who aid and abet Islamicist regimes know that they massacre gays and subjugate women. There's no one who doesn't know that Arab oil states are filthy rich and everyone except perhaps a five-year-old knows the price of gas. The Woke *choose* to be ignorant because self-imposed ignorance, they believe, is the key to paradise.

IGNORANCE IS STRENGTH

What is so jarring about Big Brother's slogans like "Ignorance is Strength" is both how blatant and blatantly untrue they are. It's hard to imagine anyone in the real world who could possibly believe that ignorance is anything other than a weakness, even after the most intense brainwashing by the most powerful of forces.

Yet, just a few years ago, a lowly schoolteacher from Waco, Texas, became a cult hero to millions declaring exactly that. His work was lauded by literary critics in the most elite of places. "Brilliant" and "sublime" were the words the *New York Times* and the *Washington Post* used to describe it. There were public readings, fan clubs and, in the epitome of irony, demands for the author to speak at the most prestigious academies of "higher learning."

What garnered such respect and acclaim for the sage, Robert Fulghum, was a slightly less pithy version of Orwell's dictum. Many millions agreed with him when he declared with an air of moral supremacy that *All I Really Need to Know I Learned in Kindergarten*.

What the five-year-old learns in kindergarten are the rules of indiscriminateness. They include not only "don't hit *anyone*," "*everyone* must be invited to the party," and "*everyone* must get a turn," but the moral and economic foundation of all Socialist theory, "every child must get a cookie but no child may ever have two."

The "strength" of ignorance was ballyhooed yet again when the reviews came in for Hillary Clinton's book of political philosophy, *It Takes a Village*. Its title is another one of those Big Brother-like slogans whose meaning Ms. Clinton made clear with the subtitle, *And Other Lessons Children Teach Us.*

Long before there was "Pajama Boy," the Democratic Socialists were known as "Flower *Children*" and the "*Children* of the Sixties" and, not coincidentally, the enemies of the movement were typically referred to as "the *Man*."

The desire to return to a place of pure naiveté is found in one of the most iconic songs of the era, "Woodstock," in which the singers repeat *ad nauseum* the Original Purpose of the Woke Supremacy, "We've got to get ourselves back to the Garden."

The idealization of the child is what led the "experts" at *Time* magazine in 2019 to scour the globe for the most important human being in the world and decide that it wasn't a doctor, scientist, inventor, statesman, artist or warrior but a sixteen-year-old petulant child with Asperger's syndrome, Greta Thunberg, whose claim to fame is that she regurgitated the banal tropes of the Supremacy about which she had not actually given a moment's thought.

Finally, it is why, before they began to call themselves the Woke, the Democratic Socialist movement was known as the "Counterculture." The goal of the Woke is not to offer an alternative culture but to counterculture itself.

The dictionary defines culture as "the arts and other manifestations of human intellectual achievement." Since these manifestations of man's intellect have sometimes been brutal – the Holocaust, for example, was an "achievement" of the intellect – the Woke are convinced that the way to prevent all future holocausts and, in fact, everything from hurt feelings and bullying to genocide, is to eliminate the intellect and destroy all of its manifestations and achievements. Nationalism is multicultural; Democratic Socialism is *non*-cultural but, before they can get there, the Woke must first be violently and destructively *anti*-cultural.

THE WOKE ARE SAVAGE

As much as the Democratic Socialists believe they've discovered a never-before-conjured and perfect ideology, the idea that paradise lay in the rejection of the intellect is not in the least bit new. In fact, the many efforts to sell the idea in the past all fall under a single, well-known, much-studied and oft-bandied-about conceit known as the "Noble Savage."

This repeatedly-rejected ideology has only this time taken root in Twentieth- and Twenty-first-century America because those who came before the Woke – "the man" – left a world so at peace and so prosperous it could afford to pay for a few generations of little savages.

The idea behind the Noble Savage is that the human being is born morally perfect and is only then corrupted by evil institutions societies have constructed such as the Family, the Nation/State and the Church. If only the Woke could destroy these cultural institutions – these manifestations of the human intellect – and throw their achievements along with all other things created by the human mind down the Memory Hole, the savage, born noble, will remain noble as he grows into his larger body and then forevermore.

Lennon's Socialist proscription of a world with no countries and no religions takes care of Nation/States as well as the Church while the Socialists' control of all possessions makes them the provider and caretaker, and thus takes the responsibilities and prerogatives of parenthood out of the hands of the adult. As in all other Socialist movements, the child in the Woke Supremacy is the property of, and is to be raised by, the Supremacists who will then instill in him the Supreme Trait which, in this case, is their devotion to ignorance.

The idea of the Noble Savage is predicated on a belief for which there is no scientific evidence, archeological record, historical support or even an iota of logic but, of course, these things are not the purview of the child or the Woke Supremacist who wouldn't have learned about science, history or logic until sometime after he'd turned six, and therefore, by his own account, has no need for them.

If the Woke were allowed to ponder his beliefs, however, he would quickly discover that the entire premise upon which his ideology is based is negated by everything else his ideology demands he believe. For example, if there is no God, then who or what created the morally perfect human being in the first place?

For the Woke to buy into their own ideology, they must reject their belief in Darwinism and reverse their rejection of the science of Intelligent Design. After all, there is simply nothing in a random universe that even hints at morality, much less perfection and, in fact, morality and indiscriminateness are diametrically opposed and mutually exclusive. There is simply nothing in "spontaneous and random mutations" that would bend towards morality, much less moral perfection. Randomness and morality are diametrically opposed and mutually exclusive, as well.

The irony is that, while the Woke have made the mere questioning of Darwinism a hanging offense –ironic in itself since even Darwin had doubts about his theories – it is the Woke who cannot logically embrace both randomness and perfection, while it is the religious (who they mindlessly ridicule as "unscientific") who can and often do embrace Darwin's work.

The believer can see God's plan in evolution. The Woke Supremacist cannot see God, a plan or even evolution. Evolution is antithetical to randomness for, if nothing is better than anything else, there's nothing to evolve into. The same is true of the human being in the Woke Supremacy; there is nothing to evolve into as people and thus permanent infantilism is their ultimate goal.

In the real world, the unacculturated savage is just a savage without culture. It is only the intellect that has allowed man to rise above the beast and create beauty and to seek truth and justice. Without it the Woke Supremacists don't end the world's evils – the Law of the Jungle is pretty ruthless – they eliminate the only thing that can overcome and defeat man's animal impulses, the intellect.

A GENERATION OF SOCIOPATHS

Almost immediately upon the arrival of the "Children of the Sixties," it became clear that a mental illness was prevalent in that population. The writer Thomas Wolfe dubbed the first full ten years of the Supremacy, "The Me Decade", and before the 70s were out, Christopher Lasch would call their illness by its name in *The Culture of Narcissism*. In his impressively exhaustive study, done with the benefit of retrospect, Bruce Gannon Gibney concluded that theirs was *A Generation of Sociopaths*.

Not surprisingly, as those suffering from this mental illness gained more and more control over society, its prevalence grew. San Diego State psychology professor Dr. Jean M. Twenge conducted a major study of the *children* of the Children of the Sixties and published her findings under the title *Generation Me* while the then-still-relevant *Time* magazine ran an extensive cover story calling them, "The Me, Me, Me Generation."

More recently, Dr. Twenge teamed up with Dr. W. Keith Campbell, an internationally recognized leader in the field of Narcissistic Personality Disorder, to complete the most exhaustive study of its kind in history and they were so alarmed by their findings, they published the work under the title *The Narcissism Epidemic*.

Just why a mental illness that had been around since the dawn of time afflicting but a very few should suddenly become first prevalent, then dominant and now epidemic during the era of the Woke Supremacy has been much bandied about with various complex explanations offered, but the reason for it is really quite simple. Narcissism is a normal and natural stage of childhood that the young, mercifully, tend to quickly pass through. Because the Woke never mature emotionally, intellectually or morally it has become the normal and natural state for them for their entire lives.

Narcissistic Personality Disorder is more than just a big ego and self-centeredness; it is a debilitating sociopathic illness whose manifestations are highlighted by a dangerously grandiose sense of one's abilities and importance, an inability to cope with alternative points-of-view, a sense of entitlement to things they haven't worked for or earned and, perhaps most devastatingly for this conversation, an utter lack of ability to empathize with others.

Believing that you are the only person in all of human history to be right and that the world will be paradise if only everybody else shared your Supreme Trait is a pretty fair definition of a "grandiose sense of one's abilities and importance." The fact that grown men and women need "trigger warnings," "comfort pets" akin to the child's teddy bear and even psychological treatment should they overhear some idea that is outside the narratives and the orthodoxies of the Supremacy hints at their inability to cope with alternative points-of-view.

It is their infantile sense of entitlement that leads the Woke to believe he can loot the fruits of other people's labor both in riots that amount to nothing other than a child's temper tantrum and onerous taxation and it is their lack of empathy that allows him to commit his crimes and cruelties against all Others.

It is this lack of ability to empathize with his fellow human being that leaves the Woke Supremacist incapable of conjuring any explanation as to why the Others might disagree with the policies, politics and practices of the Supremacy and why they can't put the behaviors of others throughout time in their historical contexts.

To the Narcissist, all understanding of the world starts and ends with himself. It starts with his grandiose sense of himself which, when combined with his bitter disappointment when the real world fails to provide him with that which he believes his greatness entitles him, ends in hatred for those who have deprived him. His failures are due to "oppression" for, to those suffering from this sociopathy, it can be nothing else.

Whatever the Woke Supremacist claims to be a product of his "compassion" (which, of course, is the greatest and most pure compassion the world has ever seen, and which anyone who has a different point-of-view is totally lacking) is, in fact, a function of his inability to empathize.

His abortion policies are formed not out of compassion for women but a lack of empathy for the child; his open borders policies or war against the police come not from compassion for the criminals but antipathy for their next victims. His siding with the socialist and Islamic supremacists comes not from his "compassion" for Muslims or people with "yellow" skin but his lack of caring about anything other than himself, the moment and The Cause that defines him as supreme.

WHO WILL LOOK AFTER THE CHILDREN?

Whether in the jungle, the Garden of Eden or the kindergarten classroom, the hatchling, the naïve and the child must always have an adult nearby to look after, protect and provide for him. This is the role the Socialist government plays for the permanently infantilized in the perfect world of their imaginations.

With all of the "possessions," the mother bird, God, the teacher or the parents, provide the food and other essentials with the little ones not even questioning, much less understanding, where the things they eat, drink, play with and everything else in their lives come from, how they were made or what it required to make them. This infantile lack of awareness was perfectly on display when the newest Supremacists decided to "run away from home" and start their own country called "Chaz." Within twenty-four hours the Woke posted a sign – in essence writing home – asking the grown-ups to provide them with the things they would need to survive.

The role of the mother bird, God, parent and teacher is one the Supremacy's Powers-That-Be gladly take on – it is, in fact, why they infantilize their followers in the first place – and it is exactly how their infantilized followers happily see them.

70

Looking at him, Evan Thomas doesn't appear to be a child. In fact, when he puts on his big boy clothes, he is the leading political analyst at *Newsweek* magazine and a favorite commentator on *NBC News*' cable showcase, *MSNBC*. He is turned to by those considered to be the most knowledgeable and experienced people in the Supremacy for his wise insights and by the rank-and-file for a way to more easily understand complex issues.

Not long ago, an example of Thomas's intellectual and rhetorical prowess was on display in a segment hosted by the network's then-top political anchor, Chris Matthews. Matthews, too, until personal issues brought about his demise, was thought of as one of the "best and the brightest" on the Left side of things. Matthews asked Thomas to provide analysis of a major political meeting that President Obama was chairing. Thomas didn't need even a moment to think before he ejaculated giddily, "Obama is like God!"

One might have expected perhaps some blowback from a serious and respected journalist such as Matthews, but he offered none. That's not entirely surprising, though, since Matthews' himself had not long before admitted that his body "tingles" in awe whenever he hears the voice of his beloved leader.

Later in the same segment, Thomas commented again. He was no less giddy this time as he chirped, *"Obama is the teacher."*

It was in a different setting that Michelle Obama offered her assessment of her husband's eight-year reign:

> *It was like having the good parent at home. The responsible parent, the one who told you to "eat your carrots and go to bed on time."*

71

Ms. Obama wasn't talking to a room filled with kindergarten children and thus dumbing down her assessment to a simile that a five-year-old could understand. She was, in fact, addressing a Leftwing *leadership* conference.

Others understand the relationship Socialists expect to have with their government, as well. Republicans derisively call it the "Nanny State" while Orwell portrayed it more like a Big Brother looking after his little siblings. The Nazis, too, had a word they used to describe what they expected of their Socialist leader. They called him "Der Fuhrer." Der Fuhrer is German for "the teacher" or "the guide."

FREEDOM IS SLAVERY

Along with God, parent, teacher, nanny, big brother and guide, there is yet one more relationship that is often used to describe the connection between the Socialist government and those it rules over. Some seventy-five years before the fictional socialist Big Brother sought to convince his followers that "Freedom is Slavery," and about the same amount of time before the German Socialists mounted the phrase "Work Shall Set You Free" at the entrance to the death camp at Auschwitz, philosopher George Fitzhugh was making a similar claim.

Fitzhugh was a proponent of both slavery and Socialism and understood them to be, in fact, both one and the same. Fitzhugh wrote that "slavery is a form, and the very best form, of Socialism." By "best," Fitzhugh meant the purest and, indeed, it is.

Fitzhugh saw blacks the way the Powers-That-Be in the Democratic Socialist movement see their followers and as their followers see themselves: "children in grown bodies," who need the "grown-up" to tell them what to do. In fact, well into the 20th Century, Democrats continued to call grown black men, "boy."

As Fitzhugh saw it, the master was doing the "children" a favor by protecting them from grown-up forces with which they could not compete and by providing them with things like food, clothing and housing that they'd never have been able to get or keep on their own. They were, in Fitzhugh's words, "far outstripped or outwitted in the chase of free competition", and thus needed the slaveowner to help them do what's best for them.

Like the modern-day socialist, Fitzhugh saw himself as the benevolent governor:

> *[A master's] whole life is spent in providing for the minutest wants of others, in taking care of them in sickness and health...*

Fitzhugh's statement, in fact, is not all that different than what the Democratic former mayor of New York – and, until his disastrous debate performance, the "savior" of the Democratic Party – Michael Bloomberg said a hundred and seventy-five years later:

> *Some people say, well, taxes are regressive. But in this case, yes they are. That's the good thing about them because the problem is in people that don't have a lot of money. And so, higher taxes should have a bigger impact on their behavior and how they deal with themselves.*

There is obviously a huge difference between chains and taxes but the Democrat then and the Democrat now use them for the same purpose: to control the behaviors of those they see as children.

Whether it's "Pajama Boy" or just plain "boy," nothing has changed in how the Powers-That-Be in the Democratic party see those they wield control over. And whether they demand you call them "Master" or insist you call them "Mayor," the Democratic party leaders still believe the "children" need them to be their parents, their Big Brother and their guide. The only difference is that this time the "children" seem to like the arrangement.

THE CONCRETE PLANTATION

The great political divide in America today is no longer between the North and South. Nor is it even between "Red states" and "Blue states." In fact, in every state across all regions, the Culture War is between those who live or work in cities and those who live and work virtually everywhere else. It should not be all that surprising, then, that, since Slavery and Socialism are one and the same, the plantations of old and the cities of today bear a striking resemblance.

For one thing, both on the plantation and in today's cities there is virtually no middle class. In all Socialist settings, whether it's China, Russia, San Francisco or the plantation, there are the very rich Master Planners and the very poor who are there to serve them and do as they say.

On both plantations, those slaves who have the strength and resources – physical then, economic now – flee to go to the "free states" where, today, they are unshackled from onerous taxation and freed from the controlling dictates of the Master Planners' regulations designed, the Master Planners swear, for their own good, but which never quite seem to turn out that way.

Left behind on both the real and concrete plantation, then, are the Master Planners and those too dependent on the meager provisions provided by those who make the plans. All the while, the Master Planners get richer and richer while doing little to no work themselves, while their slaves are never allowed to get ahead.

Not surprisingly, the Master Planners have laid out the cities to resemble the plantation in just about every way, as well. Both then and now the very rich and the very poor reside in two very different communities with vastly different amenities.

Today, there may be a few more people of color amongst the Master Planners, but, even back then, there were black plantation owners. And, of course, like then, there are still today some "Uncle Toms" of all colors willing to bow and curtsy as they say things like, "Yessum, Miss Nancy, that toilet bowl sho' is pretty."

For this, they get to live in the Big House. And the houses of the Master Planners are big, indeed. While the poor lived in shanties then and in slums today, the Master Planners live in skyscrapers, brownstones and on major estates. The Obamas recently purchased an almost fifteen-million-dollar spread amongst the lily-white folk on Martha's Vineyard and Maxine Waters somehow owns a four-point-two-million-dollar mansion located outside the poor district she rules over. Bernie Sanders, said to be amongst the "poorest" of the major Master Planners, has opted for a less opulent spread but only so that he could then buy *three* of them.

Now as then, the children of the Master Planners get the finest educations at the best academies as they are groomed to be the next generation to run the plantation, with people like Andrew Cuomo and Beau Biden virtually inheriting their positions in government from their fathers. Meanwhile, just as on the Democratic-run plantations of old, the poor are left ill-educated – if educated at all – and steeped in the orthodoxies and narratives devised by the Master Planners for their own ends.

On both plantations, the rich are protected by police departments hired by and in the service of the Master Planners, and by guns – both owned and hired – they would never allow the folks who serve them to possess. In fact, on the plantation, gun control is *always* a top priority.

Just as on the plantation of old, the poor today are pretty much left to handle their own affairs internally with the Master Planners' police showing up – neither liked nor trusted – only when the problems begin to threaten the interests of those in the Big House. So long as the riots are in the poor parts of town, the police – hired by the Master Planners – are ordered to stand down; when the Big Houses come under threat, however, the police response ordered by the Democratic party mayor is, in every case, very different.

Today, with the advent of the automobile and mass transit – the former for the Master Planners, the latter for the poor folk no longer just in the back of the bus but now the only ones on it – the plantation has spread out a bit, which is why the suburbs are now skewing more to the Left than they had in the past, but the dynamics are exactly the same.

Be it in the suburbs, the city proper or the plantations of old, the Big House is always just down the road a piece, always just far enough away so the Master Planners know that the poor folk won't be coming by at night to pay them a visit, but always just close enough for them to come by during the day to clean their toilets, mow their lawns and raise their children for them.

And, while today the Master Planners are more likely to call them "nannies" than "mammies," not even that role has much changed in the concrete plantations today's Democrats run. In fact, if one spends an hour in any park in any major city in America today, what they'll find is a nearly non-stop procession of poor people – mostly women of color – pushing thousand-dollar strollers with the babies of the Master Planners in the pram.

THEIR DAILY RATIONS

While, like Fitzhugh, today's Master Planners portray themselves as being munificent, benevolent and loving, in reality they no more want the "children" to grow-up and leave the plantation than did the slaveowners of old. As much as they may "love" them, their slaves, then and now, are their fortune and without them, the Master Planners might actually have to do some real work and be compensated not by the riches they vote themselves from monies confiscated by force but by what other people think their work is actually worth.

The social welfare programs that the Democratic Socialists have conjured and implemented over the past fifty years were never meant to help the poor move up socially or economically; why would the slaveowners want that? The majority of people who vote Democrat are the very rich who benefit from being the Master Planners, and the very poor who rely on them. The second to last thing the Planners want is for poor people to move into the middle class and stop needing them. The last thing they want is for them to get rich and move into a Big House near them.

In fact, here is how Lyndon Johnson sold his fellow Democrats on the entire Socialist welfare scheme the Master Planners have been using for the past fifty years, which they euphemistically call their "War on Poverty":

These Negroes, they're getting pretty uppity these days and that's a problem for us since they've got something now they never had before, the political pull to back up their uppityness. Now we've got to do something about this, we've got to give them a little something, just enough to quiet them down, not enough to make a difference.

According to the architect of the welfare state today's Leftists are still selling, these programs were never meant to make a difference; they were designed merely to stave off a slave rebellion by upping the meager rations doled out to those the Democrats see as both their chattel and their children.

Given that the Democratic party have been the Master Planners in every major American city for upwards of half-a-century and the problems remain – rats in Baltimore, feces on the streets of San Francisco, homeless in Los Angeles and the bodies of dead black children piling up in Chicago, for example (everywhere, it seems, except near the Big Houses) – there are simply only two things a rational person can believe. Either Democratic party policies don't work, or they work exactly as the Master Planners planned it.

THE LANGUAGE OF SOCIALISM

Orwell knew that, in order to sell Socialism to the next generation, the Powers-That-Be would have to change the meaning of words a full 180 degrees to give each new iteration of the system of invasion, oppression, enforced homogeneity, poverty, slavery, gulags and death camps a new and shiny patina. Today's Socialists understand this, as well, and thus engage in a variety of intellectual and rhetorical gimmicks so similar to the ones Orwell foresaw as to be uncanny.

One such gimmick is for the Democratic Socialist to take a concept essential to the well-being of society – concepts as fundamental as truth and justice – and insert a modifier that changes their meaning so entirely as to turn them into their very opposite.

For example, most people recognize that truth is essential to a happy, healthy, prosperous and progressing society. No matter how good one's intentions may be, if a person isn't correct in their facts, correct in their reasoning, and ultimately correct in their conclusions, even the noblest of efforts is doomed to failure.

Since the Woke Supremacist is always not just wrong but in utter opposition to all that is good, right, beautiful and true, however, they know they need to take another tack. Rather than modify their beliefs and practices in order to be correct, the Democratic Socialists change what it means to be correct to justify their wrongful beliefs and practices.

The Woke do this by adding the modifier "politically" to the word "correct." In so doing, they change what it means to be right from "comporting with fact and reason" to comporting only to their political objectives. Whether it's history, science, art or news, what the Supremacist – no matter the Supremacy – claims to be true, beautiful and right are only and always those things that advance his march toward the global paradise he imagines. That which he deems to be untrue, ugly, evil and wrong is anything and everything, no matter how well supported by reason, evidence and experiment, that in any way hinders its advance.

The Woke Supremacist, in fact, employs this same rhetorical gimmick a second time, inserting the modifiers "my" or "their" before the word "truth" and, by doing so, creates a world like that of the child's imagination where truth simply holds no agency and the rules of science, morality, beauty and justice are defined only by the "dreamer" and the version of paradise he's dreaming of.

By inserting the modifiers, the Woke Supremacist is tacitly acknowledging that he knows that what he's selling is a version of the truth that he has altered for his ideological needs. If this weren't true, he wouldn't need the modifiers in the first place. But the Democratic Socialist's antipathy for fact and reason isn't just implied. Striking is how often the Woke Supremacist comes right out and says it.

Howard Zinn – the author of the single most assigned text on America and American history in the nation's primary schools and colleges, and thus perhaps the single most influential Woke Supremacist of all – proudly and, in fact, like all Supremacists, self-righteously, declared in Orwellian fashion, "objectivity is undesirable."

Zinn then went on to explain why it is that he rejects objective facts and unbiased reasoning and replaces them in his influential works with falsified claims:

If you think that history should serve a social purpose – if you think that it should in some way advance the causes of humanity – then you make your choices based on that.

Lenin, Stalin, Mao and Hitler believed exactly that, as well. They all believed they were "advancing the causes of humanity" and, like Zinn, they all made their choices as to what to claim to be true based on that same conviction.

Falsifying history to serve a political agenda has a name. It's called "propaganda" and, from its inception, no matter the ideology, Socialists are famous for the extent of their network of lies that "advance the causes of humanity" as they each time see it.

Zinn is far from alone in publicly declaring his antipathy for the truth. Joining him in unabashedly and, again, self-righteously, acknowledging his role as a Leftwing peddler of falsehoods is one of the Democratic Socialists' founding fathers, William Ayers.

In an interview in *Sixties Radicals Then and Now*, Ayers explained the "scientific method" he employs in his work as a professor at the once respected University of Illinois:

I don't do research that involves gathering data and analyzing it. Rather, my research proselytizes.

"Research" that doesn't involve gathering data and analyzing it isn't research. "Science" that proselytizes is called propaganda, as well.

Nor is the Left's antipathy for the truth limited to just the Supremacy's historians, founding fathers and political scientists. These same sentiments have been repeatedly voiced – always with the same air of moral supremacy – by leading figures in today's Democratic party.

It was Alexandria Ocasio-Cortez – often described as the "new face" of the Democratic party – who smugly declared, "It is more important to be 'morally right'" than to be factually correct while Joe Biden, one of the *oldest* faces in the Democratic party, moralized in his campaign stump speech that, "We [Democrats] prefer truth over facts."

Finally, there are the folks in what has now rightly been called out as the "fake news." They, too, are unabashed and self-righteous as they admit to the Supremacist purposes of their efforts. A column in the *Boston Globe* publicly revealed the Supremacy's mission:

Ever since the election that shook up the world, one refrain in columns, commentaries, and social media posts has been incessant: "Now that Donald Trump is the president-elect, we cannot allow him to be normalized."

The idea that it is up to the media to decide what grown people are "allowed" to think is the same mentality embraced by Fitzhugh and Bloomberg. That they cannot allow the Other to be seen as "normal" is the same supremacist attitude forced upon Fallon and embraced by the cabaret singer Nazi-era Germany.

Perhaps the attitude of the Leftist media was best summed up by Mica Brzezinski of *MSNBC*'s *Morning Joe* when she declared in an on-air conversation about controlling the thoughts of others, "That's our job!"

The Woke "historian" has no higher calling, the woke "scientist" has no other purpose to his method, the Woke politician has no other goal and the Woke journalist has no other standard than advancing the hateful narratives of the Supremacy.

Not every word the propagandist speaks is an out-and-out lie. In fact, the best propagandists know to include just enough truth to make their stories appear plausible to those with minimal information (or who, starting at the age of six, simply don't need new information.)

Rather, the *narrative* the Powers-That-Be in these various institutions sell to those they're charged with informing, educating, enlightening and entertaining must always serve the purposes of The Supremacy. *New York Times* opinion writer Bret Stephens tip-toed (for obvious reasons) around this fact in a piece now seemingly expunged from the Internet:

> *A historian searching for clues about the origins of many of the great stories of recent decades – the collapse of the Soviet empire; the rise of Osama bin Laden; the declining US crime rate; the economic eclipse of Japan and Germany – would find most contemporary journalism useless.*

Stephens is wrong only in that he doesn't go nearly far enough. These clues – mere hints in the reporting as to what was about to happen – weren't merely missing; they were replaced by cherry-picked facts, falsified claims and wholly manufactured assertions. Like Zinn, the Supremacists in the media find objectivity to be undesirable, like Ayers they eschew gathering data and analyzing it and, like Ocasio-Cortez, they all believe it to be more important to be "morally right" than factually correct.

These reports – sometimes hundreds or even thousands of them over the years on any given story – not only failed to provide clues as to what was soon to take place;

they led those who trusted them to expect exactly the opposite of what then actually came to be.

Anyone who trusted the mainstream media to provide clues that the Berlin Wall would soon come down and that the Soviet Union was about to collapse was stunned – nothing less than stunned – when that's exactly what happened. How could anyone have been caught so unaware? After all, given that an empire doesn't collapse in a day, a week, a month or a year any more than it is built in a day, a week, a month or a year, one would expect for the professionals in the media, each sent to their various outposts specifically for their supposed expertise on the region, to have at least somewhat prepared their followers for what was soon to take place.

The reason so many who trusted the media were caught so totally unprepared for reality was that not only did the media fail to provide the clues Stephens refers to, but the media were, in fact, promoting a narrative that was the very opposite of the truth. Even as the Soviet empire was crumbling to non-existence, the narrative the Supremacists were pushing was that of a Soviet Union that was a "co-equal superpower" with the United States.

Whether these reporters were, like Zinn and Ayers, anti-American propagandists intentionally lying for the good of The Cause or simply your run-of-the-mill Woke Supremacist-enabler like Springsteen who, forced to start with the conclusion that the Soviet system was equally good and equally right, then cherry-picked and spun the evidence in an effort to tell that "true" story, is irrelevant. At this point, several generations into the Woke Supremacy, it is almost impossible to tell the liars from the merely deluded because the rhetoric and the results are the same. Either way, however, anyone who trusted the media for their information was not only left clueless, they were led to believe exactly the opposite of the truth, and being good Woke Supremacists, they then never gave it another moment's thought.

It is for exactly this reason these same Leftists failed to provide their trusting followers with even a clue leading up to the collapse of the Japanese economy Stephens mentions. Economies don't collapse in a day, a week, a month or a year any more than economies are built in a day, a week, a month or a year. Yet, even a professional historian looking back at the contemporary reporting would not find a clue to the reality of Japan's dire economic straits. In fact, anyone old enough to remember the reporting at the time will recall that the narrative the Supremacist media was pimping was that of Japan as an "unstoppable economic juggernaut."

The chasm between an "unstoppable economic juggernaut" and the decades-long recession that actually soon thereafter began could not possibly be wider. Once again, the Leftist media were not merely a "little bit off" or just "slightly wrong." The narrative they presented their followers and which their followers then accepted as reality was, in fact, diametrically opposed to the truth.

The major stories of the past many decades Stephens provides (as well as the half-dozen more I'll present forthwith) have two things in common: they were all in their narrative the very opposite of the truth, and their "mischaracterizations" all served to either overvalue another culture, peoples, government or religion and/or undervalue the United States. In other words, they all served the needs of the Woke Supremacy.

It is for this reason that the Leftists wouldn't provide so much as a clue about the rise and spread of Osama bin Laden or the drastically declining crime rates in America. The goal of the admitted propagandists was to make non-Western Islam appear to be "the religion of peace" and

Judeo-Christian America appear to be a place of crime and violence. It is the Supremacist journalist's version of making America look like a toilet bowl and calling it "art."

ALL SOCIALISTS ARE "SOCIAL JUSTICE WARRIORS"

Just as truth is "undesirable" to the Woke, so, too is justice. In fact, to supremacies, justice for all is the very opposite of what they desire. Here, again, the Woke solve their problem by inserting a modifier before the word which serves to change its meaning the full 180 degrees the Supremacy needs to cover its tracks. This time the modifier is the word "social," and, when inserted before the word "justice," it changes the meaning of justice from seeking "the closest possible wedding of outcome to behavior" to "anything, no matter how dishonest, criminal, cruel or violent that advances the causes of the Supremacy."

Because justice is undesirable to the Woke, the Powers-That-Be have rendered it impossible. The Supreme Trait of wokeness is indiscriminateness and indiscriminateness and justice are antithetical. One simply cannot be both Woke and just. In fact, when the violent Supremacists screech "No Justice, No Peace" they are making clear that there can never be peace with the Supremacy for they don't seek justice but its very opposite. No matter the supremacy, it is victory, not co-existence they seek and, whether it was Lenin, Stalin, Mao or Hitler, they seek it "through any means necessary."

There is simply no aspect of justice that the Woke Supremacist embraces. The Woke can't objectively consider the facts because objectivity is undesirable. He can't gather and analyze the evidence because his job is to proselytize. He cannot deliberate, for deliberation is just another way of saying "discriminating thought."

He cannot serve as part of a jury of one's peers because his only peers are his fellow Supremacists and he cannot render a fair judgment because everything he believes has been prejudged. In fact, not only is his verdict prejudged, but so, too is the "crime" and its punishment.

In a Supremacy, the crime one is charged with is never the crime of which they are being convicted. The crime they're being convicted of is not supporting the Supremacy. It is, in fact, the *only* crime in a Supremacy. Here, again, the Woke Supremacist publicly and self-righteously proclaims his true agenda:

> *Those who, for any combination of reasons, opposes the reformation become unwitting allies of the far political right.*

That is one of the *Rules for Radicals* written by Saul Alinsky, whose book serves as the de facto war manual for the Woke Supremacy in this Culture War. According to Alinsky, anyone who fails to support the Supremacy is summarily convicted of what is considered the greatest betrayal in all of human history – the aiding and abetting of the enemy at a time of war.

Throughout history, the penalty for treason has always been "cancellation." In less technologically advanced times, that might mean being sent to gulags, gas chambers or killing fields. With today's technology, the Woke Supremacists are more Orwellian than Hitlerian in their methods, but the difference ends there.

ALINSKY'S MANIFESTO

It is impossible to overstate Alinsky's influence on the Democratic Socialist movement. The Democratic party's last two standard-bearers were so enthralled by the man and his works that Hillary Clinton's college thesis was little other than a hagiography and Barack Obama's political strategy throughout the whole of his career has been based on a long-studied and well-executed following of Alinsky's every rule and tactic.

If Alinsky's name doesn't come up today as often as it used to it's only because his rules were so widely and deeply embraced by previous generations of Democratic Socialists that they are already baked into every word and every thought those now charged with educating the next generation to lead the Supremacy think, write, do and say. In that way, it is like what the Bible was before the Supremacy came along.

Striking about Alinsky's manifesto is that, unlike most others throughout history, there isn't even the pretense of morality in it. It is nothing other than a heartless how-to for people lusting for power and who have no moral compunction about how they get it or who they destroy along the way.

Alinsky explains the purpose of the rules in the book's first sentence:

> *What follows is for those who want to change the world from what it is to what they believe it should be.*

Given that Marx, Lenin, Mao and Hitler all wanted to change the world from what it was to what they believed it should be, according to Alinsky, the book was written as much for the next Hitler as it was for the Democratic Socialists who embrace it as gospel today.

Alinsky has acknowledged this many times, often describing *Rules for Radicals* as a sort of prequel to Machiavelli's *The Prince*, the latter being the manual on how to keep power through any means, the former on how to first get that power no matter what it takes.

Alinsky himself went out of his way to make sure this point was well understood by all. It is why, on the first page of the book's introduction, Alinsky paid tribute to the Devil:

> *Lest we forget at least an over-the-shoulder acknowledgment to the very first radical: from all our legends, mythology and history (and who is to know where mythology leaves off and history begins – or which is which), the very first radical known to man who rebelled against the establishment and did so so effectively that he at least won his own kingdom – Lucifer.*

Whatever presumption of morality the Left finds in Alinsky's vile work comes only from their shared amorality – amorality and indiscriminateness being one and the same – and from the traits shared by all Socialist Supremacists: the grandiose sense of their own importance, inability to deal well with opposing points-of-view, the belief in their unlimited entitlement, and their lack of empathy for anyone or anything that makes their ascension to power by any means necessary moral in and of itself.

Having arrived at their beliefs without benefit of fact or reason, when it comes time to persuade others in the court of public opinion, the Woke Supremacists simply have no moral or intellectual ammunition with which to do so. In lieu of actual arguments, then, when the Woke aren't violently assaulting Others, they must rely on a playground favorite to win the day. Logicians call it the fallacy of the "ad hominem" attack, but everyone else will recognize it as the childish practice of name-calling.

There are a whole basketful of names the Woke Supremacists throw at those who fail to toe the Supremacists' line – "racist," "imperialist," "xenophobe" and so on – but, as we have seen, these are all just "buzzwords," and none of them has any more moral or intellectual suasion then the insults these same Democrats used to hurl at blacks and Jews in the Old South.

The dictionary defines a fallacy as a "failure in reasoning that renders an argument invalid" and, with the Woke, it's not so much a "failure" in reasoning as it is their rejection of reason altogether.

While the names the Woke use to dehumanize the people they hate may sound more sophisticated and frightening than those one hears on the playground, they hold the same degree of validity as a five-year-old shouting at someone who hurt his feelings, "Oh, yeah? Well, you're a booger-eater." The name-calling in no way denies credence to the argument that brought on the child's emotional outburst, and what one eats or doesn't eat is wholly irrelevant to the question at hand.

Since the Supremacists have nothing beyond the buzzwords, once the "conventional wisdom" and the "givens" of the Supremacy have been pierced, all that is left to the Supremacist is to turn to another Socialist/Supremacist/propagandist, Josef Goebbels, who said, "accuse the other of what you yourself are guilty of."

The names the Supremacist call the Others are actually the description of the Supremacist himself. Thus, in the world of the Woke Supremacy, if one doesn't stand and applaud their anti-American xenophobia it's because they're xenophobes. If one doesn't buy into their anti-male sexism, it's because they're sexists. If one doesn't buy into their anti-white racism, it's because they're "racists" and so on.

There is, in fact, nothing racist, sexist or xenophobic about Nationalism. In fact, as we have seen, Nationalism is the antidote to, remedy for and enemy of every Supremacist movement of the past hundred years, which is what makes it the enemy of the Woke Supremacist today.

This is why the Woke must, yet again, reach into his Orwellian bag-o-tricks and pluck out yet another one of those modifiers. This time the Woke insert the word "white" before the word "Nationalist" and, once again, change the meaning of the concept the full 180 degrees these latest supremacists require.

A "White Nationalist" is a racist who, like the Woke, believes that all rights and protections belong only to those who share their Supreme Trait. A Nationalist believes that rights and protections belong to all citizens without regard to any other trait.

While there is a great deal of discussion these days about whether rights are equally bestowed in America and such discussion is both fair and warranted, the discussion itself proves the rightness of the Nationalist system. No such discussion occurs in Supremacist movements where, from Nazism to Wokeism, it is simply a given that the Other is entitled to none at all. A "White Nationalist" isn't a Nationalist and the Woke Supremacist knows it. If he were, the Supremacists wouldn't need to add the modifier.

THE MARGINALIZED

The Woke claim that their rejection of the truth in favor of "political correctness" and their disavowal of equal rights in favor of "social justice" is justified because they are "giving voice" to those who had previously been "marginalized." Once again (and as always) what the Woke claim and what is the truth are, in fact, diametrically opposed.

When Alinsky decreed that "those who, for any combination of reasons, oppose the reformation" are to be treated as traitors, he didn't make exceptions for blacks, women, gays, the transgendered or the transitioning. In fact, Andy Ngo, being both of Asian heritage and gay was supposedly *twice* marginalized and that didn't stop the Woke Supremacists from smashing in his skull in an effort to silence his voice.

Just as the Supremacist determines what is beautiful, true, historical, scientific, funny and everything else based on its service to the Supremacy, the Woke Supremacists decide which blacks are to have a voice depending entirely on their service to The Cause.

Woke Supremacists don't champion black people; they only champion *some* black people: those who do what the Woke Supremacy wants them to do. Blacks who, for any combination of reasons, fail to support the Supremacy by living a more conservative lifestyle, supporting a more conservative cause or voting for a candidate not approved by the Supremacy is not only as reviled and targeted for cancelling as all Others, the Woke Supremacists reserve a special and heightened degree of hatred for them based on the color of their skin. That is the very definition of racism.

To the Woke Supremacists, a black person who refuses to do as the Supremacy tells him is *worse* than the typical enemy; he is, to borrow the phraseology of another Supremacist movement, not just an "infidel" but an "apostate." He is not merely an "enemy combatant" but, according to the rules under which the Supremacy operates, he has committed the equivalent of the greatest betrayal known to man.

And, in fact, along with the most vile racial epitaphs – words that haven't been heard in America since the last Democratic party Supremacist movement in the Old South and which flow so easily from the mouths of the Supremacists in today's Democratic party – "traitor to their race" is in fact, the very charge with which the Woke Supremacists attack people of color who don't do as the Master Planners demand and stay on the plantation.

Technologies have changed, so now when the Supremacists "release the hounds" they are not, as in the days of Democrats like Bull Connor and George Wallace, actual dogs but rather trolls on the Internet hounding them but the purpose is the same. It is not a coincidence that the Southern Democrat Biden's attempts to keep a black man off of the Supreme Court was described by that man as a "high-tech lynching."

To justify their vicious assaults on people of color, the new Supremacists once again turn to Orwell. This time they insert the modifier "authentically" before the world "black," and thus their assaults are on people who "aren't really black."

While most in the Supremacy are smart enough not to say this out loud, Biden isn't one of them. It's exactly what he said in an interview with "Charlemagne Tha God" when he declared that, unless a black person voted him into the Biggest House of all, "they ain't black."

As with everything else, then – science, art, literature, journalism, history, truth, justice and beauty – the Woke Supremacist defines the color of one's skin not by objective observation or hard science like genealogy, chemistry or biology – this is why objectivity is undesirable and the scientific method the enemy of the Left – but by the one and only standard the Supremacist – no matter the Supremacy – has for anything and everything: their service to The Cause.

This is true across all of the various "marginalized" groups the Woke Supremacists pretend to care about. Democrats don't "champion women," they champion *some* women: those who support the Supremacy. Woke Supremacists don't champion gays; they champion *some* gays; those who support the Supremacy. Blacks, women, gays and anyone else who offers even one drop of support for or even compassion or empathy towards the Other immediately becomes their "whipping boy."

This is true on a global scale as well. If ISIS is good for the Supremacy, then the women who suffer under their thumb are just more "collateral damage." If gays are thrown off of roofs, then, "so be it." There is simply nothing – nothing whatsoever – that matters to the Woke Supremacist except the Woke Supremacy.

In the Democratic Party, blacks are free, just so long as they do as they're told by their master. In the Democratic party, women have the right to vote just so long as the "little lady" doesn't bother her "pretty little head" by thinking for herself. If either of them don't do as their betters order them to, they are even more viciously set upon by those who claim to be their "champions" than even the supposed "White Supremacists" with their "male toxicity."

THE HUMAN RACE

Given that thousands of black people are killed each year, the fact that the only stories the Woke propagandists report are the ones involving white shooters, it should be obvious that, when the Supremacists sit around deciding which stories to tell and which stories to keep covered up, it's the color of the shooter and not the black lives that matter.

Even more telling about the true agenda of the Supremacists is how many of these stories they've gotten not just wrong but, as with all of those other major stories of recent decades, as wrong as wrong can be. What makes their true intentions undeniable, however, are the lengths they have gone to in order to tell their fake stories. This includes editing 911 calls to make people appear to say things they didn't say, photoshopping pictures to make people appear to have done things they didn't do and altering lighting to make the participants appear to be of a different race as well as literally a thousand other gimmicks, lies, tricks and deceptions that amount not only to journalistic malpractice but likely criminality.

Consider the story that the Supremacists at *CNN* told the people who trusted them regarding the Michael Brown shooting in Ferguson, Missouri, and then compare and contrast it with what really happened. Keep in mind that this wasn't a one-day story that one anchor or one reporter on a single station "botched." The lies continued, day in and day out, for weeks on end and across all platforms.

Brown, the people were told with authority and conviction, had his hands in the air and was pleading "don't shoot" when he was "murdered" by a blood-thirsty, corrupt and bigoted cop. In other words, as always, there was no reason for the shooting. The shooter, then, was a "racist" and part of an evil and all-powerful White Supremacy.

Here's the true story.

Brown didn't have his hands in the air, and he wasn't pleading "don't shoot." Brown was, in fact, a habitual drug-user and a career bully who had only moments earlier strong-armed a local minority business owner. When he was finally shot, it was only after he'd punched Officer Darren Wilson in the face, attempted to murder him with his own gun, and was again charging towards him.

This isn't my conclusion. Those are the findings of Eric Holder, Obama's Attorney General, who investigated the case for nine months. Holder turned over every leaf, lit up every shadow and kicked over every rock trying to find something – anything – with which to keep the narrative alive. Even then, using the full authority and resources of the United States government not only could he not find a crime – any crime – that Wilson had committed, he couldn't even find a violation. Yet the Democratic Party nominee for President of the United States, Joe Biden, continues to spread this lie, and other lies just like it, to this day.

The narrative the Woke Supremacists at *CNN* and elsewhere invented involving Trayvon Martin was just as wrong and required just as much manipulation of the facts and evidence. The Supremacists were equally wrong about what actually happened at Duke University and its lacrosse team and knew it from the start. The claims of Jussie Smollett and Bubba Wallace were too obviously fake and too quickly exposed for the Supremacy to turn them into full-scale riots but they, too, were given national coverage which, until the truth finally became known thanks to alternative media, they continued to push without hesitation or correction until they found their next lie to tell.

NO LIVES MATTER TO A SUPREMACY

The Supremacists, of course, know how incendiary their fake stories are, yet, each and every time another opportunity to promote one comes along, the same people who were caught with their pants down drop their pants again.

This should make it pretty clear that, at the very least, the black lives lost in the riots that they know are likely to – and often have – follow don't matter to the folks at *CNN* and beyond. In fact, the only logical conclusion one can draw from *CNN*'s rejection of journalistic standards and their repeated use of trickery in these cases is that they *want* to incite looting, rioting and death in the black community.

For Democrats, the suffering of black people isn't their Original Purpose any more than is the suffering of "yellow" people, gays, women or even the Other. Innocent lives are simply always expendable in a Socialist system. Like anyone and everyone else, blacks who lose their lives, loved ones, businesses and dreams are just the "collateral damage" the folks at *CNN* and elsewhere brush away with a wave of their hand.

Democrats know that they benefit from black people suffering and, so long as they can manipulate the black community into blaming America instead of blaming them, they've hit the trifecta. They know that with black businesses burned and black families destroyed, blacks will be even more dependent on the Master Planners, their votes will be even further guaranteed and the discontent in the black community will grow, they hope, to the point where they'll join the violent revolution.

In fact, *increasing* discontent within the black community is another of Alinsky's written rules embraced by the Woke Supremacy:

> It is up to us to go in and rub raw the sores of discon-tent.

Special attention must be paid to Alinsky's always very carefully chosen words. Just as Michelle Obama believes it is up to the government to tell the "children" to eat their peas, Fitzhugh believed it was up to the slaveowners to provide food and housing for the "children," and Brzezinski believes it is up to the media to tell the inferior folk what to think, Alinsky's followers believe it is "up to them" to go in and foment discontent that without their agitation the blacks would be, in their mind's, too stupid to know is in their best interests.

Alinsky could not have been more clear that the "us" he's referring to are the Supremacist Powers-That-Be. This is why he said they had to "go in" to those neighborhoods from the outside. Nor could the objective of the Master Planners be more clear – it is not to make life better and alleviate the "discontent" blacks might have with America but to rub it raw. *CNN* was only doing it by the book.

The people inciting these riots aren't local people making policy in the best interests of their friends, neighbors, families or constituents; they're Supremacists working on behalf of the only thing Supremacists care about, the Supremacy. Back when Alinsky wrote the rules today's Supremacists still follow, people actually had to physically leave their Big Houses and go into these communities to incite the violence Socialists never fail to incite. Today, thanks to technology, the folks at *CNN* can sit in their studios, press a couple of buttons, and be in every home, school and business in the communities they want to see burn.

The attitude of the Woke Supremacists was perfectly summed up by *ESPN* on-air personality Chris Palmer who, when he saw the black neighborhoods being set afire, tweeted "Burn that s**t down. Burn it all down." When later the violence had reached the walls of his gated community, however, Palmer tweeted something entirely different:

Get these animals TF out of my neighborhood. Go back to where you live.

DEFUND THE THOUGHT POLICE

While the Supremacists in the media use their technical wizardry and rhetorical sleight-of-hand to falsify news stories, their fellow Supremacists in academia do the same where they rule. When it comes to race, in fact, the academics outdo themselves in their use of Orwellian gimmickry.

Faced with a scarcity of "White Supremacist" aggression, they simply insert the modifier "micro." Faced with the fact that it is only Democrats who appropriate rights, freedoms, money and basic liberties, they insert the modifier "cultural."

As always, the modifier so totally changes the meaning of the word as to turn it into its opposite. Aggressions are actions, "microaggressions" are words. Aggressions are committed intentionally, "microaggressions" unwittingly. Aggressions are intended to do harm, "microaggressions" are meant to begin a friendly conversation, no matter how awkward the attempt may or may not have been.

Most importantly, aggressions like the ones provoked by the Supremacist media in Ferguson or visited upon real journalists in Supremacist Portland, prevent individuals from doing what they wish to do; "microaggressions," at worst, hurt an overly sensitive person's feelings.

Here's how Kathy Wyle, Director of Media Relations at the once prestigious UCLA law school began an article explaining what "microaggressions" are for the institution's official journal:

> *If you've ever felt slighted or put down by something someone has said or expressed through a glance or other suggestive response, you may have been the target of something known as a microaggression.*

In truly Supremacist societies like the ones the Democrats ran in the South, the Socialists ran in Germany and the Democratic Socialists run today, the Others aren't in law school; they've been in one way or another cancelled. In Supremacist societies, the Other feels more than just "slighted," they – like Andy Ngo – feel a clawed weapon smashing into their skulls or a noose around their neck. In a Supremacist society, one doesn't have to wonder if they've been a victim or be told by their betters what it is that has "victimized" them.

Another of the Master Planners at that uber-Woke Southern California university distributed official examples of verbal "microaggressions." They included such horrifyingly acts of racism as asking someone where they're from. The school felt the need to spend time and money producing this document because, without it, no one surrounded by such opulence, grandeur and opportunity as those on the magnificent campus of UCLA would have known any reason to suspect they were "victims" of a massive and evil conspiracy that must be overthrown.

In reality, of course, there is no one above the age of five whose feelings are hurt by such things as a glance or being asked where they're from. The grown-ups telling the children the "bad words" they cannot say is just the same mind control tactic practiced by every Socialist ever, and which Orwell so brilliantly portrayed in *1984*. These efforts are nothing other than the Woke Supremacists' version of the Thought Police, and the twisted machinations of what Orwell called "Newspeak":

You don't grasp the beauty of the destruction of words. Do you know that Newspeak is the only language in the world whose vocabulary gets smaller every year?'

The purpose of this New-Newspeak is two-fold. First, with the ever-changing list of what is and isn't permitted by the "adults" in the Supremacy, rather than risk the wrath of the Powers-That-Be by saying the "wrong" thing or offending someone trained in race and gender grievance studies who will then report them to the Thought Police, people will choose to simply not talk to each other at all.

Since the same people who work to prevent speakers offering views that differ from the narratives and orthodoxies of the Supremacy from being heard on campus can't be everywhere, this self-censorship serves to ensure that unapproved thoughts aren't exchanged in more private settings like the dorm room or the dining hall. It is the same "ghettoizing" of thought, combined with the persistent effort to make the Other abnormal or subhuman, employed by the Supremacists wherever you find them.

According to Orwell, the other purpose of Newspeak is to "so limit what one is allowed to say that it becomes impossible to communicate sophisticated ideas." To those who believe that the perfect person in the perfect world is the permanently infantilized, any idea more sophisticated than that which a kindergarten child could grasp is the enemy. Indiscriminateness and sophistication are diametrically opposed and mutually exclusive. In such a world, it really is true, then, that all one ever needs to know they learned in kindergarten and everyone who disagrees with you is a "booger-eater."

SECRET CODES AND GESTURES

Even more ingenious than turning glances and greetings into grievances, is the Woke Supremacists' invention of what they call the "dog whistle." The idea behind this Supremacist ploy is that, even when the Other does and says nothing wrong, they're still evil because the Supremacists know what they "really mean."

This allows the Supremacist to declare almost anything to be a "dog whistle" since you need the grown-ups to tell you what you, yourself, didn't hear. (Just how it is that, along with the dogs, the only people who can hear it are the Powers-That-Be in the Supremacy is never quite explained.)

The Supremacists are so desperate – and believe their followers so stupid – that they've even attempted to use such things as students playing a game with their hands and children signaling to their parents that they're "okay" as evidence of a global conspiracy.

Reading people's minds, reading people's glances, reading people's hand gestures, courses invented to promote ethnic and gender grievances, fake news stories one after the other...surely, there remain racial injustices in America today; these just aren't them.

WHERE'S THE BEEF?

The real test of a "Supremacist" society is found in having the powerful actually take things away from various categories of people. This is what the Democrats did to blacks in the Old South, what the Socialists did to Jews in Germany, and it is what the Democratic Socialists do as a matter of course and design in America today.

Being told what you can say and where you can say it takes away one's freedom of speech. Crashing and disrupting meetings takes away one's freedom to peaceably assemble and the right to investigate new ideas outside of the Supremacy. Inciting riots that burn down black-owned businesses takes away people's livelihoods and even people's lives and loved ones. Taxing the poor (for their own good, of course) is designed to take away their freedom of choice. Keeping people poor takes away their ability to fund their own dreams. This is the Democratic party, from slavery through the Woke Supremacy. Those on the political right do not seek to appropriate anything from their fellow citizens nor from their neighbors overseas.

To deal with this reality, the Supremacists yet again turn to Orwell, and insert the modifier "cultural" before the word appropriation and, yet again, change the meaning of the word entirely. "Cultural appropriation" is, in fact, the very opposite of appropriation and is diametrically opposed to the concept of Supremacism. "Cultural appropriation" does not take anything away from anyone and, in fact, it gives them something no Supremacist would ever give: a compliment.

No Supremacist would take on an aspect of the culture they supposedly hate. It would be like Ilhan Omar opening a Jewish deli. In Supremacist societies like those of ISIS, Nazi Germany and the Woke, the Other is forced to take on *their* culture (or, in this case, lack thereof.)

SUPREMACISTS ARE COLLECTIVISTS

At the heart of all Supremacist movements is the single concept responsible for every act of terrorism, massacre, genocide and holocaust the world has ever known: Collectivism. Collectivism is the conviction that people should be judged and treated differently based not on their individual merits but on any number of stereotypical traits ascribed to them by the supremacy of the time's Powers-That-Be.

Not only is collectivism responsible for every great atrocity through all of human history, Socialism is at the top of the list of systems responsible for the size, scope and viciousness of these horrors. This is because collectivism, by its definition, eliminates the only things that stand in the way of such mass killings: the same due process and individual rights that Socialism destroys as a matter of course.

And, just as Socialism has been responsible for every one of the great atrocities of the Twentieth Century – the only century during which it had the power to commit such horrors on such a massive scale – every significant blot and stain on America's otherwise exceptional record of equal rights progress was not only committed by Democrats but was, in fact, the official policy of the Democratic party.

The fact that the Supremacy's historians, political scientists, journalists and others attempt to pin these wrongs on "white" people is just another example of the Left's infatuation with identity politics, collectivist ideology and their plan to divide America by race. The fact that it is accepted by the rank-and-file in the Supremacist movement is a reflection of their unwillingness to think. After all, while it is of course true that the overwhelming percentage of the people who committed these wrongs in America were white, so, too, were the overwhelmingly percentage of people who fought against them.

White people weren't responsible for these historic wrongs; Democrats were. And Democrats were because then, as now, theirs is a collectivist ideology. It wasn't "white people" who enslaved blacks; it was Democrats. And it wasn't white people who continued the violence, oppression and exploitation of blacks for the next hundred years under such policies as Jim Crow and segregation. It was the Democrats.

It wasn't "white people" whose embrace of collectivism convinced them of the inferiority of women and led them to fight tooth and nail to prevent them from getting the vote. That, too, was the Democrats.

It wasn't a "white person" who conjured and signed the Indian Removal act of 1830 or who administered those collectivist policies with such disregard and disdain for the individual humanity of the Indians that they became known as the "Trail of Tears." Those were the policies of Democratic party founding father Andrew Jackson and his successor, the Democratic party icon, Martin Van Buren.

It wasn't a "white person" who ordered the internment of Japanese-Americans based on nothing other than the color of their skin and the blood in their veins. That was the longest-serving, most powerful and best-loved Democrat of all, Franklin Roosevelt and it should not go unnoticed that it is this same Roosevelt who remains so beloved a figure in today's Democratic party that, when Ocasio-Cortez sought to sell her massive one-size-fits-all "environmental" programs to her fellow Democrats, she did so by naming her bill after the Socialist/collectivist/racist Roosevelt's signature policies, "The New Deal." That's not a "dog whistle," that's a bullhorn.

While the Woke deface monuments dedicated to Abraham Lincoln who gave his life in freeing the slaves, the Democratic Socialist responsible for one of the worst acts of racism in American history still has Democrats naming bills for him. Democrats don't fight racism; they exploit it.

Socialism has been responsible for the greatest atrocities the world has ever known. Democrats have been responsible for every major policy against women and minorities in American history. The Woke Supremacists are Democratic Socialists. They, like their party predecessors and their fellow Socialists, remain collectivists to this day.

THE DEMOCRATIC PARTY HASN'T CHANGED

So undeniable is the fact that every great human and civil rights wrong in American history is and always has been the official policy of the Democratic party, today's Democrats don't even try to bother and deny it.

Instead, the Woke Supremacists use the full array and full force of their propaganda machinery to sell a lie so ludicrous it would take no more than a moment's thought for their enablers to reject it. The tale goes something like this:

"Yes," the Woke Supremacists will admit, "the Democrats were the slave owners, and yes, of course, the Democrats were the conjurers and enforcers of Jim Crow and segregation. Yes, it goes without saying that the Democratic party used its money, resources and power to try to prevent women from gaining the right to vote and yes, well, duh, of course it was the Democrats once again who dreamt up and then implemented the Indian Removal act. The internment of the Japanese? That, of course, was the Democrats, too. In fact, every race-and-sex-based wrong in American history has been because of the Democratic party...but then suddenly, after 170 years, the darndest thing just sort of suddenly happened..."

Perhaps it was at the stroke of midnight, when the third cock crowed and the witches brew came to a boil (or maybe it was when that lightning bolt hit the village clock tower or when the pets arose from the cemetery) but sometime in 1968, every Democrat was magically transformed into a Republican and every Republican awakened to discover he'd been transmogrified into a Democrat. It was just the weirdest thing.

The inciting incident for this phantasmagorical switcheroo is said by the Supremacy's propagandists to be that Richard Nixon had had some sort of "Southern Strategy" to win the presidential election in 1968. Nixon, they say, concocted an evil scheme whereby he would suddenly alienate all of his Northern supporters, lose all of his financial backers, betray all of his friends and give up all of his personal connections and campaign staffers dedicated to the Republican party and run as a racist in the hopes of tearing Democrats away from the party they'd supported for almost 200 years, and which already had two candidates splitting the vote.

The very concept of it is ludicrous and, of course, there is no objective evidence or data that has been collected and analyzed that supports this ridiculous claim. At best, the Supremacists' admitted propagandists have a couple of "microaggressions" and "dog-whistles" and probably the fact that somewhere on the campaign trail Nixon was overheard to have asked someone where they were from.

Nixon, of course, had no more of a "Southern Strategy" than someone signaling to a friend that they're "okay" is really the secret kingpin of an international conspiracy of "White Supremacists." It's just what Democrats say because they have nothing else to say. "Racist" just sounds so much scarier than "booger-eater."

Nixon's strategy, in fact, was pretty much the same old strategy every Republican has employed for the past hundred years or more. It started with winning Ohio. As we're reminded every election night, no Republican has ever won the presidency without winning the state of Ohio. Ohio was a fiercely and famously abolitionist state whose two senators both voted "aye" for the Civil Rights Act that the *Republican* Dwight Eisenhower signed, and which Nixon, as Eisenhower's Vice President, enthusiastically supported (and which, of course, the

Democrats vehemently and violently opposed.) Nixon won Ohio.

After that, just like today, the Republican had to win in the state of Florida. With its millions of northern transplants, it's Cuban exiles and its cosmopolitan cities, it was not the kind of state one wins with a racist campaign. In fact, Florida is often thought of as *two* states, and it was the thinly populated panhandle that was considered "southern." Nixon won Florida. He lost in the panhandle.

In fact, Nixon didn't win a single state in the Deep South. That "honor" went to the collectivist, racist Democrat George Wallace. And, just as Nixon didn't suddenly become a Democrat in 1968, Wallace didn't suddenly become a Republican. In fact, Wallace remained a Democrat until his death just two years shy of the 21st century.

One of the states Wallace won was Arkansas, which would soon spawn Democrat Bill Clinton, famous for amongst other things, signing the legislation that would incarcerate blacks by the hundreds of thousands for minor drug crimes and other petty first-time offenses. That effort was led in the Senate by yet another Southern Democrat, Joe Biden.

Before slipping on the mantel of the Woke, Arkansas First Lady and Alinsky acolyte Hillary Clinton often bragged about how another lifelong Southern Democrat, Robert Byrd, was her "mentor." Byrd also just happened to have been the Grand Kleagle – the head recruiter – for the Ku Klux Klan. Byrd, like Wallace, both Clintons and Biden, never left the Democratic party.

The "big switch" narrative is no more truthful and no more accurate than any of the other tales the Woke

Supremacists tell in their history books, on the campaign trail or on the nightly news shows. The pets never arose from the cemetery; Marty McFly never went back to the future, and the parties never flip-flopped.

RADICAL CHIC

The second half of the Woke Supremacists' self-serving tale is just as convoluted and, if possible, even less true than the first. The claim is that, just prior to that eerie night in 1968, the most wonderful people who ever lived just sort of showed up out of nowhere. They were like no human beings mankind had ever known and they brought with them an ideology so new and so perfect that, if everyone could just be forced to follow along, they were going to finally lead the world to paradise. Their ideology, they declared, was nothing short of "radical."

In reality, the ideology wasn't in the least bit new, it had just been repeatedly rejected for centuries by grown-ups who couldn't didn't wish to operate only in their imaginations. Neither was the system they were selling different; it was just the same old system Marx had proposed and Lenin, Stalin, Mao and Hitler had only then recently employed. In fact, "Chairman Mao" was one of their heroes.

They were the first to call themselves "Love Children" and the first to promote the virtues of infantilization as the "Children of the Sixties" and "Flower Children" but, in reality, they were as hate-filled as the Democratic Socialists their movement would spawn. Hate was and remains the Democratic Socialist's only bond.

The Radicals were people like the terrorist Ayers and his murderous wife, Bernadine Dohrn. They were cop-killers like Angela Davis and the blood-thirsty Mark Rudd.

Joining them were the usual riff-raff of any Socialist revolution – conmen like Abby Hoffman, "red diaper babies" like David Horowitz along with, just like today, the criminal and the criminally insane who saw in the mayhem both opportunity and fellowship.

While Charles Manson was working freelance at the time, these "loving" radicals sure did appreciate his work. Here's how the *Washington Post* described the first organized meeting of Ayers' terror group, the Weather Underground, in Flint, Michigan in 1969:

> *[Their] eager embrace of terroristic violence was readily evident in the Flint meeting's mass celebration of notorious California murderer Charles Manson's gory deeds.*

It wasn't just Manson's deeds the blood-thirsty radicals celebrated; it was his purpose. Both Manson and the founders of Democratic Socialism sought to start a revolution by inciting massive race wars. It remains their goal today.

The new Supremacists didn't hide their desire for revolution:

> *Hi, I'm Bernadine Dohrn and I'm going to read to you a declaration of war.*

Nor are they any less forthcoming today about the fact that their lust for blood, vengeance and revolution has not changed. More than a decade after segueing from terrorist to a more managerial position in the Supremacy, Ayers said in an interview printed in the *New York Times*, "I don't regret setting off bombs," adding, "I only wish we'd done more."

In *Sixties Radicals: Where Are They Now?* the Leftist Ron Chepesiuk described Ayers' activities as a leader of the supremacist movement:

> *[He was] on the lam issuing communiques, exploding bombs, and trying to foment a revolution.*

Terrorism, it should be noted, is the act of *collectivists*, those innocents murdered being just more "collateral damage" in the mind of the Supremacist. It's not surprising, then, that the founders of Democratic Socialism and the Islamicist Supremacists they ally with should both then and now so readily embrace terrorism.

Now Ayers is "reforming education" and indoctrinating anti-social "social justice warriors," doing so still in the effort to foment a revolution. The only thing that has changed between then and now is that Ayers now lives in the Big House and outsources the murder, while further enslaving the "children" with a quarter million dollars of debt as a university professor.

THE HIPPIE DIPPY WEATHER UNDERGROUND

Over the years, the terrorists and murderers who founded today's Democratic Socialist movement have benefited from having the Supremacy's historians and journalists intentionally conflate the then-nascent Supremacy with that of the Hippie movement. They were in no way one and the same.

In fact, the Hippie movement wasn't actually a movement at all. It was more of a series of "super-fun" gatherings like Woodstock and Altamont, where children in fully grown bodies shunned responsibility in order to pursue such things as "free love," a free hit off of someone else's pipe and a groovy rock-and-roll show singularly popular amongst the Hippies because it was offered to them free of charge.

Sure, some people (including me) grew their hair a bit longer and marijuana went mainstream but the Hippies weren't ideologues committed to a movement; they were a band of childish young adults engaging for a short time in a super fun but unsustainable fad. They were the Pajama Boys (and girls) of their day.

Any attempt to translate the moveable party into a lifestyle and a means of self-governance – most famously on the streets of the Haight-Ashbury district of San Francisco – quickly ended in a disaster straight out of *The Lord of the Flies*. Very soon the founders of the movement themselves not only put hippieism to death with a mock funeral but did so while not in the least lamenting its demise.

The *San Francisco Chronicle* reported on what the founders of the movement called the "Funeral for the Hippies":

> *A Haight-Ashbury elder crafted an epitaph for the event: "Once upon a time a man put on beads and became a hippie. Today, the hippie takes off the beads and becomes a man, a free man.*

The radicals certainly helped promote the self-destructive, infantilizing and, in turn, enslaving ideology of the Hippie world – just as they work today to promote the self-destructive, infantilizing, and enslaving ideology of Woke Supremacism. Then, as now, the Socialists understood that it is so much easier to win a revolution when their enemies are morally enfeebled and their populace is intellectually incapable of seeing through their Orwellian tripe. The Hippies weren't the radicals;

they were the children the radicals were going to rule over, control and exploit.

The Hippies were silly, prancing children who soon thereafter grew up to give Nixon two terms and then Ronald Reagan two more, with three of the four elections proving to be the biggest landslide victories in American history. The radicals, on the other hand, were serious, hateful and violent people who never changed except in their tactics. They were from the start globalist, Socialist Supremacists seeking the destruction of their enemy, Nationalist America, and seeking to accomplish it by starting a race war. Nothing in the Democratic party has changed.

TARGETS OF THE REVOLUTION

All revolutions seek to undermine the authorities in the society they intend to overthrow –first creating chaos and then taking advantage of that chaos to come to power. Jerry Rubin – described by the *Washington Post* as a "guru of the movement" ("guru" being just another word for teacher or guide) – joined Ayers in imploring children to murder their families. Ayers screeched, "Bring the revolution home, kill your parents;" While Rubin belched, "Until you are ready to kill your parents, you're not really prepared to change the country."

In seeking to destroy parental authority the only difference between Ayers and Hitler a generation earlier was that, while the Socialist/Supremacist Ayers wanted the children to kill their parents themselves, the Socialist/Supremacist Hitler simply wanted them to turn their parents in. This was more of a practical matter than an ideological difference as Ayers simply didn't yet have the resources of the government that Hitler had, and so he had to eliminate the middleman. That government power was what he was seeking through the revolution. It's the power the Democratic Socialists still seek today.

Meanwhile, then, as now, the Democratic Socialists loved to kill cops. Clearly, the people who keep the peace were the last ones the terrorists who had just read the world their declaration of war wanted around and while "defunding" the police is less bloody, its purpose today is one and the same.

The "radicals" had their equivalent of BLM, with a direct ideological line between Leftist leaders like Rudd who chortled, *"It must be a really wonderful feeling to kill a pig..."* and the "protest" that first made second-string quarterback Colin Kaepernick a Woke Supremacist hero. The washout QB, who didn't say a word about "social justice" until he was benched, caught the eye of the Supremacy when he wore socks on the playing field that similarly depicted the police as subhuman swine, and thus righteously led to their slaughter.

These people set off bombs, murdered innocents, kidnapped and raped and, first and foremost, attempted to kick-start their Supremacist revolution by dividing and then conquering the America they hate by inciting what Manson called "Helter Skelter," and the rest of us call a race war.

THE GREATEST GENERATION

No matter how hard the founders of the new Supremacy tried, they simply couldn't find anyone from what has been rightly recognized as the "Greatest Generation" who was willing to join them in their revolutionary efforts. These were the grown-ups the "Children of the Sixties" referred to collectively as "the Man."

This was a generation forged in realities like the Great Depression of Roosevelt and the fight against the Socialist, Hitler, who then went on to build the nation's highways, cure virtually every disease man had ever known and build machines that challenged the human brain. These were the people who made sure that, for their children and forevermore, not even the sky would be the limit.

These grown and accomplished Americans had no interest in and no use for the "Children of the Sixties," with their anti-intellectualism, sense of entitlement and their pro-moting of the system they had witnessed firsthand and knew the true evils of.

Whatever America's flaws – and that generation was already addressing them with such things as the Civil Rights act of 1957 long before the radicals came along – those who had fled Hitler and Stalin to become Americans and millions more who had been sent overseas to defeat the German Socialists, wanted no part of the system the new Supremacists were peddling.

The attitude the "radicals" were up against was perhaps best summed up by the great boxer, Muhammad Ali. Having returned from a long stint training in Africa for one of his fights, Ali was asked by a reporter what he thought of the continent of his ancestors. This black man – son of the then still Democratically-controlled South who, by then, had long ago converted to Islam – said simply, "Thank God my granddaddy got on that boat."

Everyone knew that America wasn't perfect but, because they were grown-ups who had lived in the real world and not in the infantilized world of college campuses or their parents' basement, they all knew that America was, in fact, great...and getting better.

Recognizing that they couldn't find grown-ups to join their efforts, the murderers, terrorists, cop-killers, kidnappers, rapists and the mentally ill decided that their only hope was to go about creating their own people. They would, in the words of the movement's most famous poet, Allen Ginsburg, "get to you [America] through your children."

Instead of a short march through Poland like another Socialist/Supremacist, the failed revolutionaries embarked on what is known as the Long March Through the Institutions where, over time, both through natural attrition and Soviet-style purges – and often at gunpoint such as on college campuses like Columbia university – they took over the schools, news and entertainment industries (and, later, social media) and turned them into their Ministries of Indoctrination, Propaganda and Communications.

Just as the German Socialists used these institutions to create their "Hitler Youth" and the Russian Socialists used them to create their "Young Pioneers," the Woke Supremacists used these institutions to create what I call their "Ayers Youth" – mindless followers of the Supremacy so fully steep in the narratives and orthodoxies of "Democratic Socialism" and so isolated from any other point-of-view, that they would never spend even a single moment questioning them.

It was Rudd who declared that "the true flowering of the Sixties will come in the Nineties when we've taken over the institutions." Rudd was wrong only because he missed the obvious. It would take one more generation – those over whom they would rule from near-birth – to create their army of *Social Justice* warriors.

Using Rudd's estimate that one generation is thirty years – from the Sixties to the Nineties – then the generation of revolutionaries wholly raised by the new Supremacists would be coming of age and ready to fight right about...

If the hate, violence, cop killing and blood-thirsty rhetoric of today's Left seems to have suddenly come out of nowhere, it's because the Supremacists have been hiding in plain sight waiting for their army to come of age. Now they are ready to declare war yet again – Bernie Sanders even calls it "the revolution" – and they have their able-bodied and feeble-minded followers ready to kill again.

SUPREMACISTS ARE RACISTS

Of all the lies the Leftists peddle, perhaps the biggest is that they supported the equal rights movements of the Sixties and Seventies, and that it is their ideology that brought about the progress. Once again, nothing could be further from the truth. The founders of Democratic Socialism opposed equal rights with a vengeance and for the same reason the Woke do today. The last thing those whose rule is to "rub raw the sores of discontent" want – then or now – is a contented populace, and the last thing those who seek to divide and conquer want is a united citizenry.

This is why, when the newly arrived Radicals could have joined with either party, they quickly associated themselves not with the one that stood for abolition, women's suffrage and the recent Civil Rights Act but with the party of slavery, women's disempowerment, Jim Crow and segregation. It is simply a truism that people join the political party closest to their own beliefs and which is most likely to help them achieve their ends. The Democratic party, the party of national divide and racial

118

animus, was and remains the natural home for Democratic Socialists.

The White Supremacist Wallace and the Woke Supremacist Ayers had no great love for each other, but they did have a great need for each other as they shared a common enemy: The Reverend Dr. Martin Luther King, Jr. This is why, when the Civil Rights movement split into two camps – one led by King and the other by a man choosing to call himself Malcolm X – those who would eventually spawn the Democratic Socialists of today sided with the latter. In fact, Ayers and Dohrn were so enthralled by X, they even named their son "Malik," which is the Islamic equivalent of Malcolm.

Whatever King's personal musings about Socialism, his movement was in every conceivable way a Republican one. Like Republicans then and now, it was Judeo-Christian in spirit, peaceful in action and pro-American in objective. It sought *equal* rights, not special privileges nor punishments based on race.

King's movement was a Nationalist movement seeking to – and succeeding in – remedying injustice by calling on Americans to better practice their Nationalist beliefs. X's movement was in every way what the Democratic party still is today. It was Muslim in spirit, violent in action and anti-American in its purpose. X was a Black Nationalist – the modifier needed because he was the opposite of a Nationalist. He was, like today's Democrats, a collectivist, a racist and a Supremacist. When the Woke Supremacists demand that the "black national anthem" be played at football games, they are again siding with X and not King.

It made no difference to Ayers and his ilk whether Wallace promoted white hatred of blacks or X promoted black hatred towards whites; then and now, the only thing that matters to the Woke Supremacist is that there be hatred.

DEMOCRATIC SOCIALISTS ARE SEGREGATIONISTS

One policy that first drew the founders of Democratic Socialism to the Democratic party was its history of segregation. All of the aforementioned Democratic party policies – slavery, Jim Crow, the "removal" of the Indians and the internment of the Japanese, for example – are segregationist policies.

Segregation is also a hallmark of Socialism whichever ideology employs it. Whether it was exiling the bourgeoisie to frozen tundra, removing Jews to ghettos or loading Gypsies onto trains to be sent to death camps, Socialism has the same uninterrupted history of segregation as the Democratic party. It's not surprising, then, that the party of racial division and the system that requires physical divide should, when combined into today's Democratic Socialism, once again embrace this heinous practice.

While it is simply too soon for the Democratic party politicians who still need to win popular support to overtly call for segregation, in those places already run by the Democrats and their co-ideologists – places like America's cities as well as colleges and universities – segregation is once again back in style.

On the university campuses the Leftist Powers-That-Be now provide segregated housing and segregated dining facilities no different in either spirit or purpose than when the earlier Supremacist Democrats provided separate drinking fountains and separate lunch counters during the Wallace/Ayers era.

Today, with the Ayers Youth now in charge, many Leftist-run institutions have entire days when people with the "wrong" color skin aren't allowed to attend classes. These actions recall nothing if not the Democrat Wallace himself blocking the doorway at the University of Alabama. It's not that the parties have "flip-flopped" as the faux historians propagandize, it's that, while the South more and more rejected Democrats like the White Supremacist, Wallace and became Republicans, the North more and more embraced Woke Supremacists like Ayers and became Democrats.

It may have been the Democrat Wallace who said it, but it is his fellow Democrats today who have made it happen: "segregation now, segregation tomorrow...segregation forever." Not surprising, then, was that when the Woke finally had a chance to run their own "country," Chaz, it was the most segregated and racist "country" in the world.

As heinous as segregation is on its face, it typically serves a purpose beyond the mere separating of people. Segregation has always served as a precursor for the greater evils the segregationists have planned. Its purpose is to prevent the Other from disproving with their humanity the vicious narratives created about them by the Supremacy.

Thus, for example, the slaveowners segregated black and white children from each other because they knew that if black and white children got to know each other, like each other and perhaps even love each other, they would see that the narrative of blacks as "subhuman" was a lie, and the Democratic party policy of slavery would have ended in one generation.

It is for this same reason that the German Socialists first segregated the Jews into ghettos before they moved on to the gas chambers and ovens. The Socialists knew that, if they allowed the Jews to continue to live amongst the general populace, their narrative of Jews as "vermin" who could be righteously exterminated, would have been disproved by the humanity of the people's Jewish friends and neighbors.

This remains the purpose of the Democrat Socialists in segregating people today. Whether it's Jeff Zuckerberg segregating people electronically as Facebook dehumanizes the Other, or the president of Yale University doing so physically, the Woke Supremacists know that the more time people of different races spend with each other, speaking freely to each other and getting to know and perhaps even love each other, the more difficult it will be for them to gin up the hatred for the Others that the Supremacists need to sell their crimes and atrocities and bring about first the revolution and then the homogenizing of the world into the perfect "one" they all imagine.

SOCIALISTS ARE JEW-HATERS

While there have always been practical benefits for any group in using the Jews as scapegoats – most obviously their miniscule numbers combined with an unusually high level of accomplishment that lends itself to both visibility and jealousy – the Socialists' hatred for the Jew is more than a practical benefit to them; it is central to their system, no matter the ideology attached to it this time.

Although Socialism is definitionally anti-religion, Socialists don't hate all religions equally. In fact, Socialist movements always hold a unique and singular hatred for the Jewish people. It is not a coincidence that when Orwell invented a mythical character for the English

122

Socialists' requisite "Two Minutes Hate", he gave him both a Jewish name, Goldstein, and a stereotypically Semitic visage.

From the Russian Socialists' singling out of "Soviet Jewry," to the German Socialists' "Final Solution to the Jewish Problem," to today's Socialists' attempt to finish Hitler's work by strangling to death, economically, the eight million Jews of Israel through collectivist boycotts, divestments and sanctions, a singular and obsessive hatred for Jews goes hand-in-hand with the political Left.

The reason for this is simple. While all of the other religions are problematic to Socialism, Judaism is antithetical to it. Just as one cannot embrace the tenets of Nationalism and be a racist, one cannot embrace the tenets of Judaism and be a Socialist. Either Socialism must go, or the Jews must go. Thus, for the Socialist, no matter the incarnation, it's the Jews who must go.

To understand the reason for the obsessive enmity the Socialists have for Jews, it is helpful to revisit John Lennon's proscription and the three pillars required for the paradise he asked us all to imagine. Paradise requires a world with no nations, no religions and no possessions.

The Jewish people are, and even in diaspora were, a nation. Judaism is also a religion. Finally, with two strikes against them, the economic model of Socialism – slavery – is so antithetical to the Jewish creed that, when the god of the Jews first presented himself, he offered as his bona fides not such impressive credentials as the fact that he had created the universe or that he gave the world life but only that he had freed the Jews from bondage in Egypt.

For the next 3,500 years and through today, no matter the circumstances, hardships or horrors, once a year

Jews gather with family and friends to tell the story of the Jews' escape from slavery. If even one generation over the past three-and-a-half millennia had failed to do so, Judaism itself would have died out long ago. Instead, it is the longest surviving culture in human history.

That this sacred tradition has been continued unbroken for three-and-a-half millennia, through holocausts and pogroms, and every other effort to harangue, hassle, intimidate and cancel the Jewish people is beyond remarkable and shows how singularly antithetical Judaism is to the slavery that is Socialism in its "best" and purest form.

The Socialists' problem with the god of the Jews only starts with his introduction. Even before the first of his commandments is through, this god has repudiated Socialism for a second time. When he commands, "Thou shalt have no other gods before me," he renders Socialism impossible. The whole point of "no religions" is so that the people have no other gods before the Socialists and no commandments except the ones that the Supremacy decrees.

Interestingly, the god of the Jews and the gods of Democratic Socialism understand the same thing: paradise could only be man's so long as he remained naive. The god of the Jews gave man free will, and when they gained the knowledge of good and evil, paradise was lost. The Democratic Socialist has no intention of making the same mistake. He's not going to allow his "children" free will or knowledge.

Prior to the arrival of the god of the Jews, the gods were all too human. They had superhuman powers but were petty and jealous and demanded of the mortals only loyalty, allegiance, sacrifices and offerings. In other words, they were exactly like the gods of Socialism today.

The god of the Jews, on the other hand, was the first just and moral god who demanded of his creations only that they seek to be just and moral as well with no other traits or characteristics required. Since morality and indiscriminateness are diametrically opposed and mutually exclusive, the god of the Jews and those who embrace him simply have to be done away with.

The god of the Jews said, "Thou shalt not bear false witness." The Socialist/Supremacist, however, is commanded to lie at every turn and to do so no matter who or how much they hurt others. Zinn, Ayers, Ocasio-Cortez, Biden and the entire Leftist-run media proudly admit this themselves.

The god of the Jews said, "Thou shalt not steal," but the gods of socialism require that quite literally everything – all possessions – be stolen. This is why Fitzhugh understood that slavery is the purest form of Socialism, for it steals all.

The god of the Jews commanded, "Thou shalt not covet," but it is covetous that fuels Socialism in general and the Woke Supremacy in particular. These are the "discontents" that the Woke Powers-That-Be work constantly first to instill and then to "rub raw."

The god of the Jews said, "Thou shalt not commit murder," but the founders of Democratic Socialism were terrorists and cop killers who cheered wildly at their fellow "Child of the Sixties," Charles Manson's "gory deeds" and who today relish in the murder of cops and others.

Finally, the god of the Jews said to "Honor thy mother and father" but, like the people at *Time* magazine, the Supremacy honors only children (and the lessons they teach us.) Ayers and Rubin ordered children to *murder* their parents and, from day one of the movement until today, the Democratic Socialists used Orwellian sloganeering to discredit and disempower the adults, starting with "Don't Trust Anyone Over Thirty" to its modern equivalent, "Okay, Boomer!"

Those who consider the permanently infantilized to be the perfect person dishonor the mature, wise, experienced and knowledgeable adult. They honor no one who has ever lived except those who, like them, have been permanently infantilized.

The purpose of the study of Jewish scripture and other texts they consider holy is to become the best adult one can be. The word the Jews use for it is "mensch," and it is perhaps the highest compliment a Jew can give. The purpose of the study of the Woke Supremacy's sacred works is to never become an adult at all. "Mensch" is Yiddish for "man," the Children of the Sixties and the generations they've spawned hate nothing more than "the Man."

CAN JEWS REALLY BE NAZIS?

The fact that socialism is antithetical to – and thus has a singular hatred for – Judaism begs the obvious question: why do so many Jews support the party and the ideology of Jew-hatred? The answer is found in how one defines "a Jew." The question is not as simple as it sounds, and it has been debated throughout the ages by even the greatest of Jewish scholars.

This is because Judaism is a lot of things at once. It's a nation, it's a culture, it's a race and it's a religion. For this reason, it is different than any and every other religion that has ever been. It's very easy to define a Christian – he's someone who believes that Jesus Christ is his lord and savior. If he believes that, then he's a Christian, and if he doesn't, then he's not.

It is equally easy to define a Muslim. He is someone who believes that the Koran is the final testament of God and Muhammad his perfect messenger. If he believes that, then he's a Muslim, if he doesn't, then he's not.

To be called a Jew, however – even to call oneself a Jew – doesn't require any belief or practice at all. All one needs to be called a Jew is to have been born to a Jewish mother.

If there is one overriding theme to this work it is that a human being should be judged based not on the things over which he has no control – skin color, ancestry or sex, for example – or things that in no way reflect his personal choices and behaviors, such as class. These are all collective notions and the fount of every great evil the world has ever known. It is what drives the cruelties and the crimes of the Woke Supremacists today. The way to create the best world possible is to judge and treat people individually, according to those things they can control and those things that they do by choice.

The vast majority of Jews in America – and Jewish Socialists in the past starting with Marx – are not Jewish by choice (belief) or behavior (practice) but only by something they had no control over: who their mother was (bloodlines). To expect people to think and act in a certain way due to their bloodlines is not only a collectivist belief but is the very same collectivist belief that the Democrats used to justify slavery, that Germany's Socialists used to justify the atrocities they committed against the Jews, and that Joe Biden used to promote the notion that blacks who don't do what stereotypical blacks do and vote Democrat "ain't black."

In fact, these Jews-by-birth-only are well aware of the fact that they are not Jews in thought or action, which is why they typically employ yet another of those Orwellian modifiers, this time inserting the word "secular" before the word "Jew." By doing so, these almost exclusively Leftist Jews so greatly alter what it means to be Jewish as to turn it into its very opposite. The "secular" Jew is identifying himself, in the words of the Jewish scholar Dennis Prager, as a "non-Jewish Jew."

That Judaism is, in fact, different in this way is proved by the simple fact that one has likely never heard a Christian, Muslim, Buddhist or member of any other faith describe themselves as "secular." In fact, there is no such thing as a "secular Christian," a "secular Muslim" or a "secular Sikh" because it is simply self-evident that, if they're secular, they're not Christian or Muslim or Sikh.

"Jews" don't vote Democrat, *secular* Jews do – those Jews whose Judaism comes only from their bloodlines and not by choice or practice. What seems to escape the non-Jewish Jews as they support the party of Jew-hatred is that, because Democratic Socialism is based on collectivism and not choices or behaviors, if victory were to come to the revolution, it will no more matter to the Woke that he was a "good Socialist" than it mattered to the Suprem-acists in Germany that those secular Jews who supported Hitler were "good Germans."

WHY DO SOME PRATICING JEWS VOTE DEMOCRAT?

While the non-Jewish Jew makes up the overwhelming majority of "Jewish" votes the Democrats receive, there are even some practicing Jews who regularly vote for the party of the Left. Just why they do so is explained in great part by the degree of their faith and practice. Put simply, the more Jewish one is by faith and practice the more untenable it becomes to support the party of Jew-hatred and antipathy for their god's commandments.

There are basically four levels of Jewish belief and practice in America. The first is the "non-Jewish Jew" who isn't Jewish in belief or practice at all. The other three, in ascending order of practice and belief, are the Reform, the Conservative and the Orthodox Jewish communities.

For the past sixty years there has been an almost perfect diagonal line showing that the more Jewish one is by faith and practice the more likely they are to reject both the party and the policies of the Left. While non-Jewish Jews vote Democrat almost 100 percent of the time, Reform Jews do so somewhat less often; Conservative Jews less often still, and Orthodox Jews virtually not at all.

This is because the Reform Jew is barely Jewish in practice – he likely doesn't keep kosher or observe the sabbath, for example – and, while he's probably joined a synagogue, to him it is more of a local recreation center where the events he attends are to his liking because of his *cultural* upbringing. To a Reform Jew, the synagogue is likely neither a place of worship nor a school to better learn and better practice his Judaism; rather, it's more like the clubhouse at a country club but doesn't involve having to play a sport.

Most importantly, as the name of the denomination suggests, rather than using the religious texts to reform himself, he reforms the texts to suit his beliefs. Like the Leftist historian, scientist, artist and journalist, the Reform Jew starts with his conclusion about what is right, moral and ethical and then cherry-picks and spins Judaism to "prove" his ideology rather than reforming his ideology to comport to the tenets of his religion.

Conservative Jews, on the other hand, just as their name suggests, seek to conserve traditional Jewish teachings and practices. The Conservative Jew likely does keep kosher, at least in his home, and attempts to observe the sabbath. His synagogue is a house of worship and his goal is to better learn and better practice the scriptures and their teachings.

What sets the Conservative Jews apart from the Orthodox Jews is that they practice their Judaism while making concessions to the fact that they live in a secular world. For example, the Conservative Jew understands that living and working in the secular world, keeping kosher at all times is simply an impossibility and thus, while he'll keep a kosher home, he is less strict in his diet when outside of it. Orthodox Jews also hold traditional Jewish beliefs and seek to conserve traditional Jewish values but choose to do so mostly in communities of their own where they can be more faithful to its practice.

Not surprisingly, then, those Jews who reform the teachings of their bible to suit their behaviors rather than reforming their behaviors to suit the teachings of their bible are overwhelmingly likely to join with the non-Jewish Jew in supporting the party of Jew-hatred. Equally unsurprising is that the Conservative Jew is far more likely to join with his Orthodox brethren in rejecting that which is antithetical to every one of his god's commandments and which embraces policy that seeks the destruction of the Jewish homeland and the canceling of the Jewish people.

WHY EVEN SOME JEWISH JEWS VOTE DEMOCRAT

It is surprising, then, that there are even a handful of Conservative and a smattering (at best) of Orthodox Jews who pull the lever for the party of the Left. After all, they are voting for everything that is antithetical to their own beliefs, a system that was used by others to justify the most horrific of atrocities against Jews of modern times and an ideology that seeks to create a world filled only with people who are the very opposite of the menschen Judaism seeks to create.

The reason that some of these practicing Jews vote Democrat is, while every human being should be concerned about history repeating itself – that's what this whole work has been about – Jews have a long history of being used as scapegoats and the recent horrors of the Holocaust are still fresh in their minds.

These Jews see safety in the party of indiscriminateness, believing that if people don't discriminate then they won't discriminate against the Jews. Their hope is that those who do not believe in the existence of the better cannot possibly themselves be Supremacists. They subscribe to the notion that those who don't embrace judgment won't engage in acts of prejudice against them. In other words, they buy into the false premises upon which this newest Supremacy is based.

These Jews could not be more wrong. It is *exactly* the party that rejects values that is their greatest threat for, without morals, they have no moral reason *not* to engage in atrocities. If "thou shalt not commit murder (except when it advances The Cause)" is your commandment, it is simply good politics to once again scapegoat the small but highly visible Jewish population. Not surprisingly, as the Woke Supremacy has grown, so, too have their rhetorical and physical attacks upon Jews.

At the same time that these Jews underestimate the existential threat of the Democratic party of today, they vastly overestimate the threat from the political right. This is not surprising given that they, too, have been steeped in the same Leftist propaganda that turns anyone who offers even one drop of opposition to their positions into the irredeemably deplorable.

These Jews reject the party that shares their values – and even shares their god and his commandments – because they see Christianity as a *competing* religion, one that, quite frankly, hasn't always treated the Jews well, either. But that was in the Old World. Once again, America changed everything for the better.

Whereas in the Old World, Christians tended to see Judaism as a different religion competing for the souls of their children, American Christians tend to believe that Judaism and Christianity are one and the same religion and that Judaism – the religion of their lord and savior – is part of the one great story of the glory of their god.

This sea change is reflected in the fact that a never before heard phrase became the very description of American culture. Even as Jews account for a scant 2.2 percent of the population, America is understood by Christian and Jew alike – and anyone else who is honest – to be a *Judeo-Christian* culture.

It is not a coincidence then, that, along with the Jews who are the most Jewish by faith and practice, the Christians who are the most Christian by faith and practice, the evangelicals, are the biggest supporters of Jews in America and the Jewish State of Israel.

And, while those who ascribe nefarious motives to everyone and everything that gets in their way claim that evangelical support of the Jewish state and the Jewish people comes only because they're waiting for their messiah to arrive, this is just another fallacious ad hominem assault. Just because the Supremacists say it doesn't make it true and, even if it were true, it changes nothing. It's not important why someone does the right thing so long as they do the right thing. Oskar Schindler had the worst of motives for saving the Jews, but he saved the Jews.

Besides, if you're a Jew, let them wait. In the meantime, they are about the only thing standing between half of the world's remaining Jews and those in two Supremacist movements, Democratic Socialism and their allies in the Islamicist movement, who lust to finish Hitler's work. If it turns out the evangelicals are right and their messiah comes, you're going to want to become a Christian pretty quickly, anyway and, if he doesn't come, the Jews will have been saved from the political Left and its equally bloodthirsty allies in the Islamicist movements.

But that's not why the most faithful Christians support the Jews. They support the Jews because, if you have moral values, that's what you do. If you believe in the Ten Commandments, if you care about equal rights and, in fact, if you care about human rights, you side with the tiny liberal democracy of Israel and not the Supremacists who surround it. You don't side with the people who subjugate women and throw gays off of roofs; you side with the ones who had a woman prime minister all the way back in the mid-Sixties and who have and have long had gay pride parades in every town.

If you're a good person, you side with good. But the Woke aren't good people; they're *indiscriminate* people and because goodness and indiscriminateness are diametrically opposed and mutually exclusive, they side always and only with all that is evil, failed and wrong, with nothing held sacred and nothing – not even another holocaust – beyond the pale.

Finally, the Jew should feel safer with Republicans in office because, since Republicans are Nationalists, the aggrieved Jew can appeal to his fellow citizen on the basis of their common citizenship. The Jew in a supremacy, on the other hand, can no more successfully appeal to the Powers-That-Be than in Nazi Germany, Soviet Russia or any of the Islamicist states.

SOCIALISTS ARE AUTHORITARIANS

One of the most oft-heard slanders Leftists throw at those who refuse to conform to their dictates are the buzzwords "authoritarians" and "totalitarians." Because the rank-and-file never give these things even a moment's thought, they fail to see the irony of the charges.

It is, of course, the political Left that favors authoritarian and totalitarian government, while the further right one goes on the political spectrum, the more freedom from government one seeks. It's why Fitzhugh and the others understood socialism and slavery to be one and the same. In fact, the very political spectrum is nothing other than a measure of the degree of authoritarianism and totalitarianism desired by the supporters of the various systems.

Starting on the extreme Left, then, is Communism. Communism is the total (as in totalitarianism) authority (as in authoritarianism) of the state. Just to Communism's right is Socialism. Socialism is only to Communism's right – in fact, it only differs from Communism – in that it at least offers titular "ownership" of some non-essential things. Still, the prerogatives of ownership – choice – are so heavily regulated by the government and the benefits of ownership – profits – are so heavily taxed by the state that ownership is in little other than name only. Like blacks, women and everyone else, the business owner may be "free" to make some choices in the Socialist system, but only so long as those choices are the ones the Powers-That-Be want them to make.

Until recently, the totalitarianism and authoritarianism of Communism and Socialism were so far outside the political mainstream in America that not only were there few (if any) significant politicians who publicly embraced it, but people from all across the American political spectrum united repeatedly to defeat it overseas.

Today, with both the passing and the purging of old-school Democrats and the cowing of any moderates who may somehow still remain, the Democratic party is fully under the control of the extremists that Americans used to unite to defeat.

There simply is no longer such a thing as a "moderate Democrat." There is no such thing any longer as the "loyal opposition." The Democrats know this themselves, which is why they declared themselves "The Resistance" and why so few (if any) will condemn the warfare being waged against Americans today throughout and across the continent.

REPUBLICANS IN NAME ONLY

Moderate Democrats of old are now in the Republican party. Republicans even have a name for them. They call them "RINOs" or "Republicans in name only" because, before the rise of the Supremacists, their policies would have made them Democrats.

Prior to the rise of the New Supremacy, the debate between the parties wasn't *if* America was great – that was self-evident to anyone who knew anything about the real world, right down to a black Muslim boxer raised in the south. The debate across the whole of the American political spectrum was about how to continue to make America even greater.

Those in the Democratic party of old typically sought that end through somewhat bigger government, relatively higher taxes and comparatively more regulations on individuals and businesses. Those in the Republican party typically championed policies that were more local, less restrictive and came with more personal responsibility and personal reward.

Today those who seek to make America even better, no matter their stance on relative size of government, rates of taxation or comparative scope of regulations, are in the Republican party. Those who hate America and seek its destruction through, at least in the interim, authoritarian and totalitarian rule – a "dictatorship of the proletariat" – support the Democratic party. This is *not* the Woke Supremacists' Original Purpose; it's just what Socialism in both theory and practice requires.

THE NORDIC STATES

Whenever the Democratic Socialist points to a nation where Socialism has succeeded, he invariably ignores the elephants in the room of China, Russia and Nazi Germany, and references only the tiny Nordic states of Sweden, Switzerland, Denmark and Norway.

These are odd choices since none of them is actually Socialist. Not in the slightest. In fact, they all fall far to the right on today's American political spectrum. Their economic system is the same as that of the United States – free-market capitalism. They are proud Nationalists who love their country, respect the borders of their neighbors and expect their borders to be respected by others.

Believing both in possessions and countries, the Nordic States also fail the third test of Socialism. In the Nordic countries, not only does religion play a significant role in the home but it does so in the public sphere, as well. In fact, where Americans embrace the idea of a separation of church and state, in the Nordic countries religious parties – and even religious institutions – have legislative authority.

In fact, so concerned at this disinformation campaign waged by the Woke Supremacists, Løkke Rasmussen, the Prime Minister of Denmark, came to America, and told the assembled:

> *I know that some people in the US associate the Nordic model with some sort of Socialism. Therefore, I would like to make one thing clear. Denmark is far from a Socialist planned economy. Denmark is a market economy.*

Rasmussen wasn't addressing middle school students who, understandably, might not have known this simple fact; he was addressing the best and the brightest products of the Supremacy at the Harvard's Kennedy School of Government. That those who are militating for turning America into Denmark don't know the first thing about that country's economic model, governing system or culture speaks volumes about the purpose of those charged with "educating" them in the first place.

There is one more essential difference between the Socialism that the Democrats sell and the system the Nordic states employ. In the Nordic states, social welfare programs are used to benefit the people; the social welfare programs of the Democratic Socialist, like everything else in the Supremacy, are used only to help advance the Supremacy. The Nazis, Soviets and other Supremacists like the Woke use government confiscated money and power to socially engineer the world they imagine, yet the Nordic states use their programs evenly and fairly across all demographic lines.

SMALL GOVERNMENT REPUBLICANS

Just to the right of the RINOs and the Nordic states is the traditional wing of the Republican party. They are the "conservatives." These are the true liberals – lower case "l" – in that what they seek to conserve is not only America's liberal, democratic republic, but the limited role of government that allows for the freedom of choice on which liberalism is founded.

Conservatives support lower tax rates for the same reason that Bloomberg favors higher ones: they both understand that taxation is a form of control. Conservatives favor fewer federally-conjured and federally-implemented government services and fewer federally-created and federally administrated regulations not because they are – as accused by those with a vested interest in portraying them as such – hard-hearted or racist, but because they cherish for both moral and practical reasons individuality, multiculturalism and creativity.

The conservative understands that, in a nation of 330 million people, with thousands of different languages, cultures and religious beliefs and practices, on a continent with varying climates, weather conditions, topographies, soils and other natural formations and resources, the closer to local realities decisions are made the better – and the better twice over.

It is better because the locals have first-hand knowledge of local realities and then because it is the locals (right down to the family and the individual) who will benefit from, or suffer the most from, the consequences of those policies. The Socialists make policy starting from little personal and practical knowledge and with no consequences to them, which is a very bad place even for the most caring of people to start their policy planning.

Much can be understood about the difference between Socialists and conservatives by considering their very different takes on the Paris Accords on "manmade global warming." The Globalist/Socialists who all flew off in private jets to stay at five-star-hotels, typically on the monies taken from hardworking people, put together a massive one-size-fits-all global scheme to reduce carbon emissions. America was the only nation in the entire world not to sign it. America was also the only nation in the entire world to meet and exceed the reductions the scheme called for. Had Americans been forced to comply with the restrictions and the regulations conjured by the out-of-touch and wholly immune elite, Americans wouldn't have been free to innovate, create and make smarter local decisions based on local realities.

Those who seek to conserve the system that has brought the world the best of everything its ever known are called "Conservatives" and they are, first and foremost, Nationalists. Those who embrace the system that has brought the world its greatest evils, the Socialists, are almost all the way on the other side of the political spectrum.

THE LIBERTARIANS

Slightly to the right of the conservatives are the libertarians. Whereas the conservative advocates for the *limited* government enshrined in the Constitution, the libertarian seeks *minimal* government. The libertarian believes that just because the government *can* do something doesn't mean that it should.

The libertarian lives by the "No Harm Principle," which states that free men should be able to live in any fashion they desire so long as they don't do harm to others. Compare and contrast Alinsky's rules where the Master Planners "go in" and "rub raw" the sores of discontent in order to incite rioting, looting and death. Compare and contrast the Democratic Socialists' protests scripted to force others to do their will through "any means necessary" and compare and contrast Pelosi's dictum whereby the destruction of the Other is fluffed off with the wave of a hand and a mumbled "so be it."

Finally, furthest from Communism and Socialism on the political spectrum are not the authoritarians or totalitarians that the Supremacy claims but, in fact and as always, exactly the opposite. On the far-right fringe of the political spectrum are the *anarchists* who don't want any government at all.

In reality, there are almost no anarchists in America and none at all in the Republican party. There's not a congressman or a senator, a radio-talk show host or favorite columnist, a popular college speaker, stand-up comedian or anyone else in the Republican party who embraces and promotes anarchy.

In fact, those who love America are as much against the far-right as they are against the far-left and for the same reason. Anarchy would be as much a revolutionary change as the one the Woke Supremacists are attempting in turning America Socialist. This is why, just as the Woke Supremacists side with the Islamic Supremacists and why the founders of the movement sided with the White

140

Supremacists in the Sixties, the Democratic Socialists are allied today with the anarchists.

The Woke Supremacists' narrative about the "far-right" in America is exactly as far from the truth as is everything else they say. In other words, it's diametrically opposed to it. There is no "far-right" in the Republican party. In fact, even the "do no harm" Libertarian party, despite fielding a smart, articulate and accomplished candidate in the 2016 presidential election, Gary Johnson, a man who was the only reasonable alternative for those Republicans who (then) had understandable concerns about Donald Trump's lack of governmental experience, his lifelong affiliations with the people and policies of the Left and his seeming lack of decorum, could only garner three percent of the vote.

The Republican party is, in fact, so moderate that, prior to Trump, its last two presidential nominees actually came from the wing of the party that, until the rise of the Supremacy, would have been called Democrats – the "maverick," John McCain, and Mitt Romney, the only senator with an "R" next to his name to side with the Democrats in their impeachment sham.

And Trump isn't a right-winger. That's just what the Woke Supremacists call anyone who isn't a Left-wing extremist. Trump is a Nationalist like Martin Luther King; he's a pragmatist and, until the Coronavirus skewed America's priorities, he'd been doing a great job for *every* American, with the greatest gains being amongst blacks, Hispanics and women. By rolling back the policies of the Supremacist Woke he was, in fact, making America great again which, unlike Democratic party policies, was serving to *lessen* "discontent" amongst all of the people of America.

What follows is the story of four people, all of whom were beloved and even revered by the Left until they each made the "mistake" of putting moral, professional, artistic or some other value ahead of the demands of the Supremacy.

Tammy Bruce is a lifelong feminist whose intelligence, skill and passion for women's rights saw her rise to become the president of NOW's largest chapter. Because that chapter is in Los Angeles, Bruce quickly became one of the go-to people in the movement, both respected and beloved by those at the highest levels of the organization.

This all came to a screeching halt during the OJ Simpson saga when Bruce made the "mistake" of taking the side of Nicole Simpson, the oft-battered and then murdered wife of the former football star. This would seem like a no-brainer if NOW were actually a feminist organization. But because NOW is a Socialist front masquerading as a "women's rights" group, Bruce had committed an unforgiveable sin.

What happened was that the top brass at NOW had received a call from another faux civil rights group, the Socialist NAACP, who thought the story of a black man committing a violent murder was bad for the narrative the Socialists were trying to sell of a world with only black victims and white killers.

The man at the top of the NAACP ordered the women to shut up and the women at the top of the "feminist movement" did as they were told. Bruce, however, didn't. Bruce, a true feminist, refused to be a Socialist lackey and continued to use the high-profile story to call attention to spousal abuse and violence against women which, of course, is the job of a true feminist.

Following Alinsky's rule that anyone who for any reason opposes the reformation has committed an act of treason, Bruce's refusal to chuck her life's work and her moral convictions in favor of the Supremacy's demands instantly made her an enemy of the Woke. The very same people who, just the day before, had had so much respect for her, her abilities and her commitment to the cause began to savage her in the same way they savaged Jimmy Fallon for doing his job as a late-night entertainer.

Bruce, of course, was immediately sacked from her position, with the faux feminists then seeking to destroy her name, reputation and future. Bruce's first book, which tells this story as well as scores of others from her years of involvement with the political Left and at the highest levels in academia, activism and Hollywood, is called, unsurprisingly, *The New Thought Police*.

It was the same crime that saw Bernard Goldberg's nearly three-decade run as one of the most trusted and beloved reporters at *CBS News* suddenly canceled and his name and reputation attacked by the very same people who testified to his honesty and integrity just twenty-four hours earlier.

Like Taibbi, of *Rolling Stone*, whose quotation started this work, Goldberg had long been aware of the corruption and malfeasance in the media and he, too, "tip-toed" around it for years. He'd bring it up now and again when the examples were so egregious it was hard to remain silent but the people who were committing the egregious acts, of course, were not the least bit interested in his calls to higher professional standards. Their failures weren't "lapses;" they were the things people do by design in a Supremacy.

Finally, with nowhere else to turn, Goldberg wrote an article detailing a particularly blatant example of "fake news." Goldberg was savvy enough to take that example from another network so as not to betray his colleagues at *CBS.* This made no difference to them, however, because Goldberg had betrayed the Supremacy as a whole.

Almost instantly, Dan Rather – later axed for being exposed for using forged documents to try and steal the 2004 election for the Supremacists – declared Goldberg to be a "right-wing fanatic." It is an odd charge given that, until that moment and for twenty-nine years, Rather had tacitly testified to Goldberg's trustworthiness by throwing to him on some of the biggest stories *CBS News* sought to portray as "the truth."

Goldberg was not only run out of *CBS*, but, despite his nearly thirty-years of experience at one of the world's largest news outlets, he never again landed another fulltime job on any station, network or newspaper – national or even local – except for a short stint as a sidekick on a little watched *ESPN* chat show.

Perhaps most telling is the story of Larry Summers, the then-president of Harvard University who was cancelled for the crime of introducing science into a symposium on...wait for it...science. The buzzword the Supremacists used this time was "misogynist."

Obviously, until then, Summers had done an outstanding job of keeping his misogynism well-hidden as he made his way up the ranks of dutiful Socialists all the way to the very top of his profession. Of course, the crime he was charged with and the crime he'd actually committed were two very different things.

I'll let the Left-of-Center *Atlantic* magazine tell the story from its article, titled: *Why Feminist Careerists Neutered Larry Summers:*

Like religious fundamentalists seeking to stamp out the teaching of evolution, feminists stomped Harvard University President Lawrence Summers for mentioning at a January 14 academic conference the entirely reasonable theory that innate male-female differences might possibly help explain why so many mathematics, engineering, and hard-science faculties remain so heavily male...

... Summers's suggestion—now ignominiously retracted, with groveling, Soviet-show-trial-style apologies—was that sex discrimination and the reluctance of mothers to work 80 hours a week are not the only possible explanations for gender imbalances in the math-science area. He noted that high school boys have many more of the highest math scores than girls, and suggested that this might reflect genetic differences. He also stressed the need for further research into all three possible explanations.

The foul brute may as well have rapped that women are "hos," or declared that they should be kept barefoot and pregnant. The most remarkable feminist exercise in self-parody was that of MIT biology professor Nancy Hopkins, who famously told reporters that she "felt I was going to be sick," that "my heart was pounding and my breath was shallow," that "I just couldn't breathe, because this kind of bias makes me physically ill," and that she had to flee the room because otherwise "I would've either blacked out or thrown up."

No doubt, Summers should have offered this grown woman a "trigger warning," provided her with a "comfort pet" and then paid for her psychological counseling before offering a perfectly reasonable scientific theory

145

which didn't comport to the narratives and the orthodoxies of the Supremacy.

The only thing the *Atlantic* got wrong in the report, in fact, is that rapping that "women are 'hos'" is something the Supremacists actually champion because, according to the Supremacy, misogyny is "authentically" black.

There is yet one more story of a favorite of the Left going in an instant from revered as a hero to being declared a "right-wing fanatic," a "racist" and a "sexist" with every conceivable effort then made to destroy his name, reputation and his works. His name is Donald Trump.

Trump was in the public eye for almost half-a-century before he ran for president. During this time, he was beloved by the same people who now want you to believe that he's the Anti-Christ. His friends, colleagues and fans included Oprah Winfrey, who was one of the first to suggest he run for president, Hillary and Bill Clinton who attended his wedding, and fellow New Yorkers, Chuck Schumer and even Al Sharpton.

Trump worked for a decade with the same folks at NBC television who now swear that he is evil incarnate. In Hollywood, a Donald Trump cameo in a movie or TV show was a coveted prize yet now, suddenly, they've deemed him to be Beelzebub. The same hometown papers that helped make Trump a legend for the first five decades of his adult life decided in an instant to tell their readers that Trump is really – and has always been – the spawn of Satan.

The man they now call "racist" received the Ellis Island Medal of Honor alongside Rosa Parks and Muhammad Ali for his contribution to civil rights and, in fact, the Ali Foundation itself honored Trump at their annual gala dedicated to recognizing "people who are making significant contributions toward securing peace, social justice and/or human rights."

Any serious consideration of Trump's policies and politics makes clear that he isn't a "right-wing fanatic." In fact, many of the most vocal members of the "Never Trump" movement oppose him not because he is too far right but because he's not conservative enough for them.

Trump is a pragmatist who simply wishes to get great things accomplished. This is why he has been able to get along so well with the people he had to get along with to be successful in New York, and why he's accomplished so much in his numerous and varied careers including the phenomenal economy he built before the Chinese virus put it on hold.

Trump isn't a "racist" or any of the other buzzwords those in the Supremacy use to attack their enemies any more than was Bruce, Goldberg or Summers. That's just what the Supremacists say because they have nothing else to say. The "crimes" he's committed aren't the crimes he's charged with. In a Supremacy, they never are. The "crime" Trump has committed is that he opposes this latest Globalist/Socialist/Supremacist movement.

When the Woke Supremacists call Trump and his supporters "racists" they don't mean that the President's policies in any way put blacks, Hispanics or anyone else at a disadvantage. Quite the opposite; like the knife and fork, because America's way *is* better, everyone who embraces it is in turn advantaged. In fact, Trump's policies have seen the greatest gains specifically amongst the same women and minorities that the Democrats have disappointed for half-a-century and for a hundred years before that.

Trump's "crime," like Fallon, Bruce, Goldberg and Summers before him, is that he puts something – in this case America and the American people – ahead of the Supremacists' agenda.

CONCLUSION

The world as we know it – so prosperous that "poverty" now means someone who is richer in real terms than kings and tsars and popes of yore; so without hunger that millions turn down food every day because it isn't "vegan" or "whole" and so without war that for the past half-century, the only people to have worn a uniform in America are those who have volunteered to do so – begun 100 years ago when America first introduced Modern Nationalism to the world.

Since then, the only impediment to the growing peace, prosperity, freedom and even further progress on all fronts and across all lines (including racial) has been Socialism and the other Supremacist ideologies they invariably ally with. The only places left on earth where injustices are systemic and institutionalized are those where Socialism or one of its fellow Supremacist systems reigns.

The election this November is bigger than any specific program, the relative rate of taxation or comparative size of government. It's a referendum on two systems: the one embraced by Marx, Lenin, Stalin, Mao and Hitler which Orwell warned about and that is showing its purpose and efficacy in Leftist-run cities, states and institutions across America and the Nationalist system recognized for over a hundred years as the friend of freedom and equality from India to Selma, Alabama and from Hong Kong to the Middle East and the font of prosperity and progress that not even its detractors can deny.

It is a referendum between a system that always promises paradise and always through the same means: a world homogenized into one, with one-size-fits-all policy administered by Master Planners who believe themselves to be god, parent, teacher, big brother, nanny, slaveowner and Fuhrer all wrapped into one and those who believe, even if they haven't always perfectly practiced, that all people are created equal with rights that are inalienable.

Just as before, then, Americans must put aside their partisanship and their personal interests and, across all races, sexes and ideologies, come together to fully repudiate this latest Socialist/Globalist/Supremacist system. Just like in the past, once that existential evil has been dispatched with, Americans can return to their debates about how best to make America even greater still.

A victory at the polls will not end the Culture War. The Supremacists are simply too entrenched in the schools and universities, newsrooms and entertainment fields as well as across the whole of the massive social communications industries to be so easily vanquished. What is to be done about them is something that is essential we think about and plan for.

As much as I had intended to end this work with specific suggestions as to what must be done and a call to action to do them, it has been suggested to me by people I trust and respect that this is not the moment to do so. With the election just seventy-five or so days away, looming like the landing at Normandy, to distract from it with detailed plans about what is to come next, they convinced me, was neither wise nor prudent.

Besides, just exactly what those plans would be will be determined as much by the outcome three months from now as the battle plans for after Normandy depended on the outcome of that operation. I promise that, soon after the election results are known, to revisit this work and provide my thoughts on what can and must then be done.

In the end, as with that other Globalist/Socialist/ Supremacist movement that sought to homogenize the world and create the perfect society of their imagination, Democratic Socialism must either be totally defeated or we will live in a Cancel Culture where not even as good a Warrior for the Cause as Matt Taibbi is any more than but one infraction away from being cancelled themselves.

This Culture War is just the latest, and perhaps last, battle in the war between two diametrically opposed and mutually exclusive systems of governance. What life on earth will be like for the next hundred years and well beyond that will be as much determined by which side wins as it was when Nationalism fought Socialism in every one of its previous incarnations.

Made in the USA
Coppell, TX
03 September 2020

36598571R00087